GHOSTS OF BOULDER

GHOSTS OF BOULDER

ANN ALEXANDER LEGGETT &
JORDAN ALEXANDER LEGGETT

FOREWORD BY WENDY HALL, CARNEGIE LIBRARY, BOULDER

HAUNTED America

Published by Haunted America
A Division of The History Press
Charleston, SC 29403
www.historypress.net

Page 7: Watercolor by Carol Hume Davis.

First published 2013

Manufactured in the United States

ISBN 978.1.60949.736.1

Library of Congress CIP data applied for.

Notice: The information in this book is true and complete to the best of our knowledge. It is offered without guarantee on the part of the authors or The History Press. The authors and The History Press disclaim all liability in connection with the use of this book.

For Nicola, Joan, little Sara, Jane, Pam, Valerie, Steph R., Steff G., Maysie, Liz, Scott and Nic…you all know why.

A house is never still in darkness to those who listen intently; there is a whispering in distant chambers, an unearthly hand presses the snib of the window, the latch rises. Ghosts were created when the first man awoke in the night.

—J.M. Barrie

CONTENTS

FOREWORD

I have enjoyed working with people researching ghost stories for the past twenty or so years. Each person is seeking something specific—a clue that no one spotted before, a detail in a floor plan to an unknown room or some new twist on an old tale that will now turn heads when told. My job is to hunt through all of our archival records, whether they are from books, clippings or a collection of old letters and photographs stored in a box just waiting to be discovered. All of these items help to tell the story, no matter what type of story it is. The author's job is to investigate these wonderful artifacts, interpret their meaning and spin them into a great story that will entertain you, the reader.

Everyone enjoys a good ghostly story. We want to have our doubts raised, as well as the goose bumps on our arms and the hair on the nape of our neck. The stories in *Ghosts of Boulder* are no exception. They bring up questions as to what really happened in each of these homes and businesses or to these characters. The interesting twist to these stories is that Ann Alexander Leggett and Jordan Alexander Leggett took the time and energy to fully research each entry, from the original owner to the current resident, oftentimes interviewing people associated with the story. Following on the success of their earlier books, this mother-and-daughter team proves that no stone goes unturned.

From its early founding in 1859, the town of Boulder, nestled in the foothills of the Rocky Mountains, has been the source of numerous tales, both real and tall. Boulder seems to make it in the papers quite often, much of it due to the uniqueness of the people who live or lived here. Many stories of Boulder's illustrious past have attracted the attention of readers interested in learning more about the eccentricity of this town. This volume is sure to entertain readers, as well as raise a few doubts in the minds of those of you looking for a good mystery.

Wendy Hall, Manager
Carnegie Branch Library for Local History
Boulder, Colorado, 2013

ACKNOWLEDGEMENTS

Thank you!

To Jane Carpenter, our intrepid and talented editor, researcher and hand-holder. Thank goodness you are a night owl. You are *the best*!

To Wendy Hall of Boulder's Carnegie Branch Library, who always knows where all the good stuff is. And thank you for the wonderful foreword!

To Krista Socash, who is a rock star for being our go-to psychic.

To Abby Daniels of Historic Boulder, for her enthusiasm and support.

To Becky LeJeune of The History Press, for helping us keep our ducks in a row.

To The History Press, for asking us to write another one.

To all of the people who were willing to share their stories with us.

To all those close to us who understand that we are crazy but put up with us anyway. We love you all.

INTRODUCTION

It's been more than eleven years since I coauthored the *Haunted Boulder* books with Roz Brown. I never dreamed that ghosts would be a recurring theme in my writing, but then again, I never thought I would ever eat an oyster. So there you go. Life certainly is a fascinating journey.

In 2011, after being approached by The History Press to write for the publisher, I coauthored *A Haunted History of Denver's Croke-Patterson Mansion* with my daughter, Jordan. That book covered the rich history of the house, in addition to the stories of the spirits that reside within its walls, just as the *Haunted Boulder* books did. That seems to be our formula. It's our theory that from the history come the ghosts. After all, it's more fun and truly frightening to find a connection between the ghost activity in a structure and those who actually physically inhabited the place. Anyone can make up a ghost story, but when you back it up with history—now, that *really* makes your hair stand on end. So, most of the stories here are full of great history.

After finishing the book about the Croke-Patterson Mansion, we weren't so sure that we ever wanted to write about ghosts again. That book stuck to us, if you will. The mansion still finds a way to lure us back, and it keeps us within its ghostly grasp. We were done. Through. But lo and behold, The History Press then asked us to revisit the Boulder ghost scene. We couldn't resist, and in doing so, we found a few more gems that are sure to please both the lovers of history and things that go bump in the night. In addition, we updated a few of the chapters from the original two *Haunted Boulder* books (and added a few new ones), and thus, *Ghosts of Boulder* was born.

Krista Socash, our go-to psychic, joined us again to give us her interpretation of some of the structures. Krista is a professional clairvoyant, spiritual teacher and healer. She provides training for people interested in developing their psychic abilities and spirit-to-spirit communication. When Krista is around, things just look different; it's always a good time. You can contact Krista at specialkspirit@gmail.com.

I'll end this the way I started, with the journey bit. The last eleven years have certainly been a roller coaster ride of sadness, hope, trauma, joy, persistence and rejuvenation for me personally. But there is one thing that has made it all worthwhile: the absolute honor of working with my very talented daughter. Life is good.

Oh and by the way, if you have any ghost stories you'd like to share, we'd love to hear them (ann@oceangirldesign.com). See? We just can't seem to break away!

We hope you enjoy *Ghosts of Boulder*.

Ann Alexander Leggett

THE DECKER—TYLER HOUSE

In 1987, when Kathryn Howes, a transplanted preservation architect from Washington, D.C., first set foot in the Decker-Tyler House in north Boulder, she knew that she had to have it. Despite the home's disrepair and the look of disbelief on her husband's face, she knew that she belonged in the house. Her every sense told her that it was meant to be hers and that her family was destined to restore the house to its former glory. Since that first day, Kathryn has felt a strong connection to the Gothic Revival farmhouse that was once the home of Clinton M. Tyler and his family. She has also felt the presence of spirits that seem to watch over her.

During Halloween week in 1999, as part of Historic Boulder's Spirit Tour, visitors were treated to a tour of the home led by a psychic from Psychic Horizons. A gentle breeze rustled the branches of the redbud tree (the oldest in Boulder) that still arches over the walkway. The lights in the jack-o'-lanterns flickered, making the pumpkins with their wicked smiles seem to laugh at those who passed by. The visitors were in for a treat as they learned about the spirits that roam the house, so beautifully restored by Kathryn and her husband.

Built in 1874, the Decker-Tyler House sat on eighty-three acres of prime farmland, bought by Clinton Tyler from Judge J.H. Decker. Early photographs show the home as the only structure standing for miles around in north Boulder. Architect E.H. Dimick, who designed the University of Colorado's Old Main, also designed the Tyler home, which now stands out as the only historic building in a sea of '50s ranch houses. As one of Boulder's

The historic Decker-Tyler house, circa 1886. *Carnegie Branch Library for Local History, Boulder Historical Society Collection.*

earliest pioneers, Clinton Tyler had great foresight for the opportunities the area had to offer. Known as a generous and highly energetic man, he was one of the city's wealthiest citizens, with interests in livestock, agriculture, construction, sawmills, real estate and even politics. At the time of his death, his holdings reportedly included more than thirteen thousand acres of land throughout seven Colorado counties, including one thousand acres in Boulder. His financial interests extended to what was then the territory of Wyoming as well.

In 1860, Tyler came to Boulder from Wisconsin with his wife, Sarah, their firstborn child, Lillian, and Tyler's father-in-law and family. They originally settled in Black Hawk, drawn to the area by the promise of gold. There he ran a six-stamp quartz mill, the first of its kind in the state, brought by wagon on his journey from the Midwest. Designed with large cylinders that crushed the ore, some stamp mills of the time were very transportable, and Tyler's was one of the largest in the area. He ran his own custom mill, and this income formed the base of what would become a vast fortune.

In addition to his milling interests, Tyler was also known in the area as a patriot. During the 1864 Indian scare, he was the first man to answer the call for volunteers to protect citizens from Indian raids and was commissioned by Colorado territorial governor John Evans as a captain of the Third Colorado Calvary. Called the "100 Days Men" and the "Rough and Ready Tyler Rangers," the group provided protection normally supplied by the U.S. Army. With the soldiers away fighting the Civil War, the Indians had greater opportunity to reclaim their tribal lands and uproot the miners and other settlers. Not only did Captain Tyler ride with the unit, but he also furnished many of the horses ridden by the men.

Tyler is also credited with the construction of Boulder Canyon's first toll road, linking Boulder to the mining communities of Central City and Black Hawk. This was a major undertaking given the geography of the canyon. Tolls were collected at two stations on either end of the road. One dollar was charged for each wagon and train, seventy-five cents for carriages. No toll was collected if travelers were on the road to attend a funeral or church services.

In 1872, the family settled in Boulder, and Captain Tyler quickly established himself as a well-respected citizen. His connections with the University of Colorado (CU) are legendary. Local historians say that on a blustery winter night in January 1875, a weary rider approached the Tyler home. The Honorable D.H. Nichols had come from a meeting of the territorial legislature on most urgent business. Several Colorado towns were being considered for the establishment of public institutions. If Tyler would promise the initial funds of $15,000, "an institution of higher learning" would be awarded to Boulder. Tyler pledged his support, gave the rider a fresh horse and sent him on his way. And the rest, as they say, is history. The main campus of the university was founded five months before Colorado was admitted to the Union in 1876.

In 1884, Tyler was appointed a regent of the University of Colorado. His family, which had grown to include five sons and three daughters, continued its ties with the university. His daughter Ella was the first woman to graduate from the school in 1886, and her husband, prominent Boulder lawyer Richard Whitely, was in the school's first graduating class, in 1882, consisting of only six men. Tyler's son Bert was also a student at the university but tragically died of meningitis at the age of twenty-one.

Captain Tyler, astride his big bay gelding, was a familiar sight in Boulder and the surrounding towns. He was frequently away for days on end, while his family waited for his safe return. In those dangerous early days of Colorado towns, houses were often built with an "Indian tunnel," a long underground tunnel leading to an outer structure that would allow the family to escape in the event of an Indian attack. Tyler's grand house was no exception. The entrance to the tunnel is still located in the cellar of the home, but it has never been explored by Kathryn or her family.

Whether he had ridden his great horse off to attend to his many business ventures or to fight the Indian Wars in the late 1800s, it's as though the house today still waits for Tyler's return. The spirit of a woman, possibly his wife, waits at the top of the main staircase. She is one of the most prevalent energies in the home, and Kathryn has often felt her friendly presence. Whether it is a change in air temperature or currents, Kathryn senses an almost nurturing feeling that seems, at times, to come out of nowhere.

Psychic Krista Socash visited the home before the night of the Historic Boulder Spirit Tour to do an interpretation of the house. She went without any prior knowledge of its history or what Kathryn had been sensing. She, too, felt the woman on the stairs. "She is very happy that Kathryn owns this home," Krista said. "She is very pleased that Kathryn is here."

Immediately upon entering the house, Krista turned around toward the front door through which she had just entered and saw the apparition of a big bay horse staring back at her through the screen. "I felt the very strong presence of a big horse that seemed very loyal to its owner." Upon hearing this, Kathryn was eager for Krista to see a historic picture of the home, framed and hanging in the kitchen. It was an old photograph of the house, clearly depicting three of the family's horses standing outside near the front door. "These must be the horses you are seeing," Kathryn said, pointing to the photograph. But Krista pointed out another horse in the photo, a large bay standing to the right of the others. Kathryn was surprised. "I had lived in the house with that photo on the wall for twelve years," she said, "and I had never seen that horse in the photograph."

Krista's visit brought other presences to light that Kathryn had long suspected inhabited the home. The energies of two young girls playing in the upstairs hallway were very prevalent—perhaps the spirits of the Tyler daughters. During the Historic Boulder Spirit Tour, Kathryn and Krista said that a young boy apparently pulled away from his parents and wandered up the stairs. In the middle of Krista's discussion about the home, the boy returned and asked in a frightened voice who the two young girls were whom he had seen playing in the upstairs hallway. He had actually seen the spirits, as many young children can.

Krista was also drawn to one particular room in the home from which several strong presences emanated. What is now an extra upstairs bedroom felt to Krista like it had been used as a healing room, or a room where

Katherine Barth stands on the stairs of her home, where the spirit of a young woman has been seen. *Photo by Ann Alexander Leggett.*

sick people in the Tyler family had gone to recover. In those days, children and adults often shared sleeping quarters. Seldom were people able to be relocated to convalesce in a hospital when they were ill, nor did they have the luxury of taking medication for a speedy recovery as they might today. Therefore, some homes had an area or a room where those who were ill could be separated from the rest of the family to recuperate. Surprised by what Krista sensed, Kathryn mentioned that ever since they had moved in, she and her husband had called that room the "healing room" and had slept there whenever they felt ill. They, too, had sensed the room's therapeutic spirits. Krista also felt the energies of a sick young boy in the room, as well as an older woman who sat looking out at the lights of Boulder through the window. She said that a feeling of death, one that felt like a miscarriage, was also prevalent in the room.

When another psychic visited the home with Krista, he revealed the presence of another spirit. Upon entering what is now the dining room, he immediately pointed to a corner where a large armoire sits. "I feel the energy of an unhappy African American man in the corner, and I see something having to do with water." Unable to make sense of the feeling, he and Kathryn looked at the home's original blueprints. To their surprise, the blueprints showed that the corner had once been the location of the sink in the original kitchen. Interestingly enough, the 1885 census report lists one household domestic living at the home.

In the spring of 2013, we revisited Kathryn at her historic home. She had asked for us to come by again and bring Krista because she was feeling as though the energy in the house had shifted or changed somehow. She wanted some insight. Immediately upon entering, and as soon as we had greeted one another, Krista moved to the circular stairway and looked down. "I need to go to the basement," she said. "The basement needs attention." Kathryn had set out tea and treats, and we chatted for a while first, but we could tell that Krista was anxious to get downstairs. As we sat in the living room, Krista noted that the spirit of Mrs. Tyler seemed to be at peace but that she still watched over her house. The spirit was comforting and soothing and spoke through Krista with words of support for both me and for Kathryn. She spoke of being impressed with us, wishing that she could have accomplished in her life all that we had in ours. However, bound by the world as it was then, she could not. She had arrived as soon as we sat down, and then, having spoken through Krista, she left just as quickly as she appeared. We didn't see her, but we felt her, just as Kathryn always has throughout the years.

But the basement still beckoned, and down we went. Visiting the basement, with its dirt walls and narrow passageways, was like stepping back in time. Little had changed down there since Tyler's time, with the exception of storage shelves, the heating and plumbing works and some insulation. The "Indian tunnel," long since cordoned off by Kathryn, seemed to call to Krista, and that's where she went first. Standing at the entrance, she felt so many memories from prior years. Thoughts and visions of the past went through her mind, and she asked Kathryn questions in a rapid-fire style. The visions were not hostile or angry but instead played out in Krista's head like an old-time movie reel. And all of the things Krista said had some historical basis in the house. So Kathryn's supposition was true: things had indeed changed since the last time we'd visited. This time, the energies seemed to Krista to be calmer and waning.

Spirits aside, perhaps the most intriguing part of this story is the research that Kathryn herself has done—research that may hold the key to the strong attraction she feels to her home. The actual geographical paths of westward migration of both her grandmother's family and the family of Clinton Tyler were very close, down to the same town in one instance. Kathryn's research on her family shows that her grandmother on her father's side was a Tyler and supposedly a distant relative of the tenth president of the United States, John Tyler. Her grandmother's family came from New York and New Hampshire, eventually settling in Clinton, Iowa. Clinton Tyler's family traveled from the East Coast to Wisconsin, where the rest of Kathryn's relatives lived, and then settled in Clinton, Iowa, before their journey westward. Is Kathryn a descendant of the Clinton Tyler family? Has she come full-circle to own a home that, unbeknownst to her, was once inhabited by her own relatives? The woman on the stairs seems to think so.

HAROLD AND EDITH

William and Mary Newland once owned much of the Newlands neighborhood in north Boulder. Originally from Pennsylvania, in 1871 William Newland homesteaded 240 acres, where he farmed wheat, ran a herd of dairy cattle and grew some of the city's most delicious strawberries. Newland died in 1886, and in 1890, his wife, Mary, an enterprising businesswoman, built the grand Newland mansion that still stands on the corner of Dellwood and Broadway. She lived in the house until her death in 1906.

Now one of the most desirable places to live in the city, the Newlands area boasts an eclectic mix of homes, including 1950s split-levels, new Craftsman-style houses and many small, traditional homes that have been remodeled and expanded to generous proportions. Located west of Broadway, bordered by Alpine on the south side to Hawthorn Avenue on the north, the tree-lined streets of Newlands form a tidy grid. Originally platted in 1891, north–south streets were numbered, while the east–west streets were called avenues, starting with First Avenue (now Alpine) and increasing, numerically to the north, to Sixth Avenue (now Forest). A map drawn in 1910 shows Sixth Avenue to be the northern limit of Boulder. As the neighborhood expanded and became more populated, lively civic debates began in 1952 to redesignate the avenues with names from nature. Then as now, Newlands neighborhood folks formed an active neighborhood association with a variety of events designed to promote a sense of community. It has been successful.

The Grape Street spirits were quiet once a psychic cleansing was done. *Photo by Ann Alexander Leggett.*

An elderly couple had lived in the little house on Grape Avenue since it was built in 1956. One of the only streets in Newlands that is not perfectly straight, Grape Avenue wavers slightly at intersections, interrupted by small medians and disappearing for a block before resuming, gently curving around original property lines at the former edge of town. A small, wood-frame house was centered on the lot and painted white with a lime green band of siding around the bottom half. The property was always neat and tidy, with the lawn meticulously mowed and edged, and the rose bushes in the back were legendary in the neighborhood. The inside of the house was comfortable and clean. A workbench in the basement was arranged in an orderly fashion, with all things kept in their place. Harold and Edith were very proud of their home and it showed.

But time passed quickly. Boulder changed and the couple grew old, and after thirty-eight years in their beloved home, Edith died in the house in 1994. Heartbroken, Harold also died in the house, outliving his wife by only six months. The house was sold at an estate auction, and Harold and Edith's aging neighbors watched in wary anticipation as the house changed hands.

Michael and Elizabeth were thrilled with their new home. The energetic young couple, while appreciative of the home's perfect condition, wanted to make some changes to suit their lifestyle. On their first night in the house, they set about tearing up the shag carpets to see the condition of the hardwood floors hidden underneath. Old blinds came down, and new paint colors were chosen. Walls were marked for removal. They worked for months. Bathroom fixtures were changed, the kitchen was updated and some of the original doors were replaced with archways.

But the work didn't just stop inside. Ecologically minded, the couple tore out the grass in the front yard and replaced it with xeriscaping, flowers and trees. The new colors and textures in the yard were spectacular, and the little house looked very different. They even removed Harold's long-tended roses in the backyard, believing them to be incompatible with the new contemporary landscaping. Slowly but surely, the couple worked on the interior and exterior until the house reflected their personalities and became comfortable for them. Little did they know when they started the transformation that they would be disturbing the house and that the previous owners were not going to be happy about it.

After work one evening, the couple, while sitting in the bright living room, heard a strange sound. *Squeak, squeak, squeak.* What in the world was that noise? They turned from their chairs to see the hanging leaf of the pine table near the kitchen wall swinging back and forth on its own. Was a plane flying overhead, causing a vibration that made the leaf move? Was a breeze blowing through an open window? The cause was not obvious, so they wrote it off as odd and forgot about it.

However, a few days later, the leaf began to move again, and this time they paid more attention. Elizabeth immediately sensed a connection to Harold. She realized that the table with the moving leaf was directly above his workbench, which still stood in the basement. She also realized that she and Michael had redone everything that he and Edith had worked so hard to maintain. Unsure of what they were experiencing, let alone what to do about it, they mentioned it to a friend with psychic powers, who agreed to come by.

A few days later, their much-anticipated remodeling work in the basement was set to begin. Paintbrushes in hand, they descended the stairs. At the bottom, however, they shouted in unison as they reached the last step. Both of them, at the same time, felt excruciating pain in one of their knees. "It was just too strange," Elizabeth says now. "We couldn't believe it happened to both of us at the same time." They went back up the stairs, and the pain subsided. They knew for sure now that something was amiss in their house. Michael would experience the knee pain several more times when entering the basement, which quickly became an unpopular place to go.

"There is someone else living here." Those were the first words from the mouth of their psychic friend, Carol, who had come by for dinner. According to Elizabeth, Carol immediately walked to the basement steps and looked down. Elizabeth told her about the knee pain, and Carol wasn't surprised. "The man's spirit hasn't left the house," she said. "If you want to help him move on, we can do that." Elizabeth and Michael agreed, and with that, they scheduled a time for Carol to come by for a house-cleansing ceremony.

Several days later, they all took a seat on the floor of the living room. Carol had burned sage in all the rooms of the house, and they were ready to begin. She spoke to the spirit and told him that it was okay to move on, and at the end of the ritual, she rang two small bells, one in each hand. Immediately after ringing the bells, the house transformed. "I never sensed that the house had a heavy feeling before," said Michael, "but it suddenly felt so light. There was a tremendous rushing feeling from the floor to the ceiling, and we got chills. We just sat silently for a few moments, unsure of what was going on. It was incredible. It definitely felt as though something had left the house."

Sitting in their colorful kitchen discussing the events that unfolded in their house, the couple began to recognize just how much they had offended Harold by their makeover of his precious home. Perhaps with the many transformations in Newlands over the years, and after the loss of his beloved Edith, old Harold had finally had enough of change. But all is at peace now in the house, and his spirit has apparently moved on.

THE ARNETT—FULLEN HOUSE

Tucked away at 646 Pearl Street, the Arnett-Fullen House seems to beckon to passersby. A curious Victorian-in-miniature, the little yellow house with the French mansard tower and gabled roof sits back from the street on a corner lot, bounded on two sides by a most intricate wrought-iron fence. With its elaborate gingerbread trim, arched windows and quirky porches, the two-story structure is an eclectic if not classic example of the Gothic Revival style. In front of the little house, the original stone stepping block used to board a horse-drawn carriage is still somewhat intact. Constructed with the finest materials of the day, the house was built in 1877 by Willamette Arnett, a flamboyant businessman who delighted in owning what would become a city showplace. Nothing like it existed in Boulder at the time.

Will Arnett came to Colorado as a child in 1859 at the age of fourteen, his family lured to the area by the gold strikes near Pikes Peak. His father, Anthony Arnett, immigrated to the United States from France in 1828. An astute businessman, the senior Arnett acquired interests in a variety of local ventures, including mining and real estate, and was one of the University of Colorado's earliest contributors of both land and funds. He owned more than two hundred acres of land in the area, on which he ran horses and cattle. His holdings extended from what is now Columbia Cemetery to the center of the CU campus, south to Baseline and all the way west to Gregory Canyon. He also owned several lots on Pearl Street, where he eventually built the structure that would become the Arnett Hotel in 1876. The popular

The Arnett-Fullen House, circa late 1800s. *Boulder Genealogical Society, Martin R. Parsons Collection.*

hotel, originally a large public hall, was transformed into a hotel in response to the housing needs associated with the mining boom. Well respected and known about town as an honest man, Anthony Arnett was a true pioneer of the city. His family with wife Mary included nine children. Will was one of only four who survived to adulthood.

Will had his father's ambitions in business but unfortunately not the success. As a matter of fact, local historians have noted that the two were often complete opposites. Married twice and with two children, Will had a reputation for being extravagant and flashy. He was a walking picture of flamboyance, right down to the ten-dollar gold pieces he wore as buttons on several of his suit coats.

In keeping with his character, nothing was too ornate for young Mr. Arnett as he set out to build his home and livery on Pearl Street. The finest craftsmen in the area were hired, and no costs were spared. Designed by George E. King, a prominent local architect, the layout of the 1,885-square-foot house hasn't changed much since 1877; it still includes a parlor with a large bay window on the lower floor, a dining room, a family bedroom, a servant's bedroom, a kitchen, a pantry and a china closet. A bathroom, with hot and cold running water, set townspeople abuzz, as these amenities were a first for Boulder. Trompe l'oeil painting and ornate floral designs adorned the entry hall and parlor. Four small bedrooms made up the upper level. For the cost, the house was on the smallish side, but what it lacked in size, it made up for in elegance.

One of the focal points of the interior of the home is the narrow, winding stairway, visible immediately upon entering, rising to the upper floor. Wide enough for only one person to pass at a time, it is framed with an exquisite black walnut balustrade complete with a stunning rosewood and bird's-eye maple inlay. It is on the bend of this stairway that one of the home's spirits is most often seen.

In February 1877, the *Boulder County News* wrote this about William Arnett's new home:

> *The exterior of Will Arnett's new residence on west Pearl is so nearly completed as to show the architectural beauty of the building in which it excels any residence ever before erected in Boulder. Mr. Arnett delights in the beautiful, is always ornamenting his grounds, and even his stables. The entrance to his livery stable is painted and gilded till it looks like an art gallery. But this new residence is his pet ornament and the gem of the city.*

The house certainly brought notoriety to Mr. Arnett, just as he had hoped. It was not without its bizarre tales, however. Some say that sometime before the turn of the century, Will's mother fell into a coma and "died" from overtightening her corset. A funeral was scheduled, and her body was laid out for viewing in the northwest corner of the house. Apparently, at the last minute, Will noticed some movement in his mother's body and loosened her garment. To the astonishment of all who were present, the poor woman immediately revived.

Building costs of the home were said to total $4,000, almost double what a similarly sized home should have cost at that time. For the ornate wrought-iron fence, Will spent $1,500 in shipping costs alone, having had it delivered by rail and by oxen all the way from Pittsburgh.

Unsurprisingly, the house acquired a great deal of debt. Construction liens on the home began to accumulate, and financial woes caused Will's business ventures to falter. The collapse of the silver market in the early 1890s hit Denver and surrounding mining towns particularly hard, and the great Panic of 1893 was perhaps the last straw. Will headed for the Northwest in the late 1890s hoping to strike it rich in the Klondike Gold Rush. He died almost penniless in Dawson City, Yukon Territory, in 1901.

Historical records and local reports vary on the actual dates of occupation of the home's next few residents. It is believed that Eliza Jane Fullen bought the Arnett House as an investment in the early 1900s. Eliza was the widow of Hiram Fullen, a Boulder miner, with whom she had three sons. She rented out the gingerbread house for several years before moving in with her mother, sister and children. She spent her last years in poor health, resting in the small bedroom on the main floor with her sister, Lilly, at her side. After Eliza's death, Lilly became the main resident and caretaker of the house. Eventually, declining in health and in finances, Lilly moved into a local nursing home. The Arnett-Fullen House began to fall into disrepair.

In the 1960s, one of Eliza's sons, Hiram Fullen Jr., moved in and, with his wife, set about restoring the house to its original splendor. The task was not an easy one. The balustrade of the stairwell had been painted black, completely hiding the stunning woodwork, and in some rooms, as many as fourteen layers of wallpaper adorned the walls.

It's not clear exactly when the ghost activity in the house began. In 1993, the property became the home of Historic Boulder. Alan Hafer, the organization's executive director from December 1998 to June 2000, felt the spirits on several occasions, most often during the day as opposed to the night. Office staff jokingly referred to "the ghost" whenever

The original stepping block used to board carriages is still in place in front of the historic Arnett-Fullen House. *Photo by Ann Alexander Leggett.*

office snafus and computer failures occurred. It soon became apparent, however, that the equipment glitches happened at moments that were just too coincidental to be accidental. The staff during Alan's tenure believed one of the spirits they were sensing was that of Will Arnett himself. Items disappearing into thin air overnight would provoke desk-clearing searches the next morning, to no avail. Once, when furniture was being rearranged in the offices, the staff joked that Will would not be happy with the change. At the exact moment of the comment, a window shade fell from its mountings. Some staff members described sudden temperature shifts in a room or the feeling of someone being in the room with them when they were clearly alone.

Alan Hafer recalled a story that further convinced him that there were active spirits in the Arnett-Fullen House:

> *Four months after I started at Historic Boulder, I was going through my desk, and I found a box labeled "Jack's Bones." No one in the office knew what they were, and we all laughed about a box with such a name. Finally, we decided that they were bones that archaeologist Jack Smith had dug up at an old Boulder stage station. We cautiously opened the box and found what appeared to be an ancient pig and deer bone. I set the box on the table in the front office so it could be returned to Jack. But overnight, the box disappeared. We tore the office apart the next morning, but it was nowhere to be found. We never did find those bones. Just as they appeared in my desk, they disappeared. Will has them someplace.*

Later, it was established that no one on the staff had sent them out or taken them. "Jack's Bones" were never seen again.

With its rich history and resident spirits, the Arnett-Fullen home has been a perfect candidate for several Historic Boulder Spirit Tours over the years. Mary Bell Nyman, director of Boulder's Psychic Horizons, visited the house before one such tour to do an interpretation. When she first entered the house, she immediately sensed the spirit of a girl on the staircase. "She was standing on the stairway, and she appeared to be approximately thirteen years old," Mary Bell said. "She was wearing a white-ribbed blouse, and she was quite delighted to be noticed. She wanted people to feel her energy."

The ghost of the girl on the stairs is the most well-known spirit in the house and perhaps in the city. On the night of the tour, as visitors entered the home, Mary Bell was surprised that the spirit of the girl stayed on the steps the entire night. Her energy was evident by a feeling of cold that the visitors could actually run their hands through. "She clearly loved the attention," Mary Bell said. "She had a positive, happy energy."

During the tour, a visitor took several color photos of the house as Mary Bell spoke. When the visitor saw the developed photos, the one of the stairway had a white blotchy patch. Thinking that it was simply overexposed, she threw it away. Later, when she realized that the overexposure could have something to do with the spirit, she retrieved the photo from the trash. At second glance, she saw that the energy had revealed itself on the film, winding its way up the stairway.

Anthony Arnett, Will's father, circa 1899. Anthony is thought to be one of the spirits in the home. *Carnegie Branch Library for Local History, Boulder Historical Society Collection.*

But who is the girl on the stairs? Alan Hafer had heard stories of a woman who died of pneumonia in the home. According to Hafer, her weeping, wheezing and crying could be heard throughout the house. Her death was quite prolonged and very painful. Hafer feels that the spirit on the stairs may be the woman returning at an innocent age. Could it be Eliza Jane Fullen?

According to the folks at Historic Boulder, another spirit lurked in the home as well. The presence of an older man was felt on many occasions by the office staff, who sensed his spirit in the southeast corner of the old dining room. Some refused to sit in that area of the home because they felt uneasy. "I immediately sensed a heavier energy in the back," Mary Bell said, "very much like that of an older, gruff man, perhaps a disapproving father."

After talking to the Historic Boulder staff after the tour, Mary Bell made the connection of the spirit to Anthony Arnett, Will's father. Prudent and hardworking, the elder Arnett was known to have been very upset by his son's profligate lifestyle. Others believe the ghost is that of a CU professor who lived in the house with his young student wife, causing quite a scandal

The current owners have been refurbishing the Arnett-Fullen House to its original state for the past eight years. *Photo by Ann Alexander Leggett.*

at the time. He was said to have died in the house. According to psychics, an area of cold air frequently surrounds his spirit.

Mary Bell's interpretation of the spirits in the house answered questions for the staff at Historic Boulder and confirmed their suspicions. "It wasn't scary for them in the least," Mary Bell said. "It was a validation of what they had been sensing for quite some time."

In 2005, the house once again became a private residence, and the owners embarked on an extensive restoration. Years later, they say that the house is relatively quiet and perhaps happy that "things are being put back the way they should be" through the restoration process. The quaint little Victorian at 646 Pearl, still in the process of being refurbished to its historic elegance, is sometimes a featured house on the Historic Boulder Spirit Tours, much to the delight of those ghosts that sometimes roam the narrow hallways.

THE GHOST OF WILLIAM TULL

The events that unfolded on a warm summer evening in June 1867 are the makings for one of Boulder's oldest ghost stories. Only the winding banks of Boulder Creek near the Broadway Bridge can tell the true tale of William Tull and his demise. His spirit didn't rest for many, many years. That much is known for sure.

Legend has it that twenty-six-year-old William Tull was a good kid. Originally from Ohio, Tull was raised with Chief Niwot's tribe of Arapaho Indians, and he became an adopted member of the band as they roamed the West. When the Sand Creek Battle of 1864 nearly decimated the tribe and killed its chief, Tull moved into the town of Boulder to look for employment. He found work as a ranch hand on the north Boulder spread of James Tourtellote. Despite his move, his friendship with the remaining members of the Arapaho endured, and he frequently visited them as they moved from camp to camp.

Tull worked hard for Tourtellote, and one summer day, having earned some time off, he asked his employer for the use of two horses to visit Arapaho friends camped at the Cache la Poudre River near present-day Fort Collins. (Some historians say that Tull was off to visit his Cheyenne Indian bride.) Tourtellote granted his request, and with one horse saddled for riding and the other packing supplies, Tull headed out on his trip. His first stop was Burlington, a heavily used stage stop south of what is now known as Longmont. There he bought groceries and continued on his way, arriving at the Indian camp the next day to the delight of the tribe.

The spirit of William Tull is said to wander the path along Boulder Creek. *Photo by Ann Alexander Leggett.*

Tull had apparently promised Tourtellote—whose brother, George, was a prominent Boulder merchant—that he would return on a specific date. When that time passed, rumors of horse theft spread, and a posse was formed. Trackers followed Tull's path north to Burlington and then on to the Indian camp, where he surrendered quietly. According to legend, the tribe's chief told the posse that Tull meant to leave earlier but had only recently recovered his two horses, which had run away with the tribe's wild herd. The explanation fell on deaf ears.

Frontier justice was swift and final in the West. Even with officially appointed local deputies, the authority of a U.S. marshal might be several days' ride away. Local citizens might decide that justice in the territorial court was too slow and ineffective and take matters into their own hands. Early in 1864, a group of citizens calling themselves the Montana Vigilantes had formed a brutal posse in the lawless mining town of Virginia City, in what was then Idaho Territory. In little over a month, twenty-two men were summarily hanged by the posse for alleged crimes ranging from highway robbery to horse theft. It was later rumored that one man was hanged simply for objecting that some of the previous victims may have been innocent.

Horse theft in particular was considered a gravely serious crime met with no tolerance. Men caught committing the crime were often hanged on the spot without the benefit of a trial. To make matters worse for William Tull, it was a time in Colorado when tensions between white settlers and prospectors and the local Indians were as high as ever. A young white man raised by Indians and with an Indian wife might fall under even more suspicion.

Tull was escorted into Boulder by the trackers and was placed under arrest in a room guarded by Deputy Sheriff Anderson. Apparently, the town had no jail at that time, so Tull and his guard holed up in a room above the blacksmith shop. Tempers ran high that night, and soon a mob formed. Storming the blacksmith shop in the dark of night, they wrestled Tull from the deputy and led him to the banks of the creek. Throwing a rope over the low limb of a cottonwood tree, they hanged young William Tull for a crime for which he had not been tried, a crime many came to believe he had not even committed. After Tull's death, it was revealed that Tourtellote had probably sold him the horses. If that was the case, Tourtellote's motivation for reporting them as stolen is lost to history. Rumor has it that proof of the sale was found among Tull's effects after his death.

The citizens of Boulder awoke the next morning to witness the aftermath of what was Boulder's first and possibly only lynching. As he hung from the cottonwood, William Tull's feet scraped the rocky ground below as he slowly suffocated during the night. It was a tortuous death. An uproar among the town's citizens ensued. The Arapaho tribe, upon hearing of their friend's untimely death, threatened revenge. Fearing an Indian attack, the townspeople hastily built a fort at the rear of what eventually became the First National Bank. The threat was never carried out.

While his grave was being dug, Tull's body was laid in the home of Ephriam Pound, located just east of the town's dairy. Citizens, including schoolchildren and their teachers, crowded the home to view his corpse. He was finally laid to rest on the slope of the Pioneer Cemetery, also called Lovers' Hill Cemetery, on Sunset Hill.

The cemetery, which was used from approximately 1867 to 1870, held the remains of about twenty-four individuals. The main plot was located on the top of the hill, while the pauper section was down on the slope. The only cemetery in Boulder at the time, Pioneer Cemetery was nothing more than a wind-swept bluff overlooking town. There were few headstones or markers, and citizens of the town had long been outraged at the disrespect shown the dead. Most of the graves were eventually moved to the more fashionable Columbia Cemetery on the corner of Ninth and Pleasant Streets.

In 1935, local historian Martin Parsons wrote of his experiences in the cemetery as a young boy, indicating that the story of Tull's lynching in 1867 persisted in local folklore for more than fifty years after he was hanged and laid to rest: "I met Granville Berkeley in the cemetery one summer, and he showed me the grave of William Tull. He had marked the grave with three large cobblestones. Tull's grave was the farthest down the slope. There were several graves higher up. The last time I was there in 1924, I counted twenty-two graves on the top of the hill but couldn't locate a grave on the slope of the hill."

While doing roadwork in 1940, the City of Boulder, not knowing that graves still existed in the area, unearthed the skeletons of an adult and a child. There is no record of Tull's remains ever being found or moved to the Columbia Cemetery.

With his death by hanging, William Tull's story was far from over. It is said that after the lynching, his unhappy spirit rose to meet a Boulder judge and a friend as they walked along the creek. To their horror, they saw the image of a man hanging by the neck from a cottonwood tree. Unable to comprehend what they were seeing, they moved closer to the tree, but the vision of the man drifted away, only to reappear standing near the creek. The ghostly figure carried a rope and motioned toward its mouth as if it was in pain. According to the men, the apparition then disappeared into the evening light.

William Tull's ghost was seen a few days later by a local constable and again by a doctor, both of whom witnessed a man hanging from a tree limb, fading from sight as they approached. Additional sightings reported Tull's ghost approaching people walking along the creek and motioning, as if asking for help in removing the rope around his neck. The story of the ghost quickly spread through town, perhaps fueled by a sense of guilt over the hanging of an innocent man.

As joggers and bicyclists cruise along the creek path today, they are most likely unaware of the events of that fateful night in June 1867. Traffic rolls by on Broadway, and life in the town, now a city, moves at a fast clip. Perhaps the restless spirit of William Tull has finally found peace, or maybe not.

SALT BISTRO

Push open the heavy, eight-foot door of Salt Bistro on Pearl Street, and you've already touched a piece of the past. That door used to be floor joists, more than a century old. What has that floor absorbed in the last century (literally or figuratively)? Make your way over to the Mermaid Bar, warmly sculpted out of local walnut and festively adorned with a reclining siren, and have a seat. Your bartender will guide you through a choice of craft cocktails, hors d'oeuvres or entrées, supplying you with the requisite silver as you go.

But then you notice it: one end of the bar, tucked almost out of the way, already has a place fully set—silver, glasses, plates and napkin—as though someone had a special place set just for them, always ready should they desire it. You see it again on your next visit, a lunch meeting, and your late evening date the next time as well. After a few meals or Salty Hour samplings, during which that place setting is never occupied, you finally have to ask the waitstaff who merits that seat. The response may surprise you or make you grin, but it will certainly send goose bumps up the back of your neck: "We kept that place setting at the bar for the spirits, out of respect." While the spirit activity at Salt is kept mainly out of the dining room, the history of that building is rather rich. It began its life, if you will, in 1883 as Trezise & Sons Undertaking.

John Trezise was born in London in 1856 to a miner named Edward and his wife, Alice. After Alice's death, Edward ended his mining career in Cornwall and ventured across the pond to America. Beginning in

California, Edward made his way across the country and up the ranks until he was superintendent of Delaware Mines in the copper-producing region of Lake Superior. His family joined him there, and they all found their way to Central City, Colorado, in 1871. Edward began milling there and stayed until 1896, when he moved to Boulder to take over his son John's ranch.

John was, at heart, the quintessential entrepreneur, so well suited to Colorado in the late nineteenth century. Having picked up the essentials of undertaking from spending time with an uncle, he started his own undertaking business before he had even turned seventeen. By the time he retired, he had established branch offices in Idaho Springs and Denver, acting as their manager until he grew too ill for business. Over the course of his prestigious undertaking career, Trezise dabbled in jewelry, furniture, groceries, livery and ranching to boot.

Trezise left Central City in 1886 for Cornwall, England, to recover from an illness believed to have been brought on by his exhaustive ambition. He married there and brought his wife, Georgiana Tyack, back to Colorado, where they settled in Boulder, chosen for its lower altitude and related health benefits. They had a son, John Albert "Bertie" Trezise, who died on October 30, 1891, after living only eighteen months. From 1893 to 1902 and again from 1908 to 1912, John Trezise held the elected position of coroner of Boulder County. Having won the office by margins previously unseen by any county election in Colorado, Trezise was renowned for his professionalism, efficiency, public service and dependability. He was affectionately known as "Popular Johnny," the people's favorite. Before holding that esteemed office, and even before electricity came to Boulder's Pearl Street, he owned and operated Trezise Undertaking at the corner of Eleventh and Pearl, followed quickly by other embalming outfits in the nearby towns of Erie and Louisville.

Embalming has a long history, reaching back even before the Egyptian practice of mummification. Closer to Trezise's lifetime, however, the practice was still an inexact science. Formaldehyde wasn't discovered until 1867 (by a German chemist), and before then, arsenic and alcohol were among the various materials used to preserve the dead. The intent of the practice was to keep bodies from decaying until they could be buried at home, particularly if the decedent had died fighting abroad or had moved away from the family homestead. By the close of the nineteenth century, however, embalming had become more mainstream and readily available among even the westernmost areas of the United States. As a result of this shift in funeral practices, by the time Trezise

Left: Undertaker and prominent Boulder citizen John Trezise, circa 1899. *Carnegie Branch Library for Local History, Boulder, Colorado.*

Below: John Trezise (in doorway) in front of his undertaking business at Eleventh and Pearl, circa 1899. *Carnegie Branch Library for Local History, Boulder, Colorado.*

was in office as county coroner, business was booming, so to speak. This allowed him to not only open more offices but also install himself as a more influential part of Boulder business and commerce. Even so, he never forgot to take care of the public, who allowed him to remain in such an estimable office.

Trezise was a well-known member of numerous groups in Boulder County (almost every fraternal order, in fact), and as one of Colorado's first embalmers, he found himself to be central to the funerary trade as the turn of the century approached. Famous for owning beautiful dapple-gray horses and luxurious carriages for funeral processions, he also was found using his broughams to give ladies from the Woman's Christian Temperance Union lifts home or to various outings. With perhaps a little less tact, he offered rides around town to the elderly on a regular basis. Each Thanksgiving, he donated dozens of turkeys to those less fortunate, and he offered relief to the bereaved at every turn. Trezise was succeeded in the office of coroner in 1912 by his assistant, Leslie Kelso, and Trezise died on Halloween in 1918. People remembered him for his kindness and generosity, his professionalism and his extensive service to the public. Georgiana continued the business for a few years after his death.

Trezise & Sons Undertaking occupied a beautiful brick building at the northwest corner of Eleventh and Pearl, on the west end of today's popular tourist attraction: the Pearl Street Mall. Trezise used to pull his carriages up to the Eleventh Street side to unload bodies by the stairwell that led to the basement of the structure, to the embalming room. The basement level was lit naturally for the duration of its first year of use until electricity was introduced to Boulder in 1887. A series of window wells and grates at once provided light to the lower level and discouraged the collection of debris in or around the windows. The curved brick layers that once capped the window casements are still visible just above the sidewalk today, although those apertures and the stairway have since been covered by concrete. Future owners of the building would find themselves competing for space with unknown energies in the basement, possibly trapped beneath that concrete.

In the fifty years between the end of John Trezise's era as Boulder's county coroner in 1912 and the building's next-most exciting chapter as the infamous Tom's Tavern, quite a few momentous events took place. Pearl Street was the first street in Boulder to be paved, in 1917, and the first traffic light was installed in Boulder at the corner of Twelfth (now Broadway) and Pearl in 1937. The Great Influenza of 1918 claimed

Trezise among its thousands of victims in Colorado, leaving Kelso and mortician A.E. Howe to serve alternating terms as coroner several times. Georgiana Trezise kept his business going for a few years after his death, and then she died in 1947. Finally, in 1962, the building fell into the capable hands of Tom Eldridge.

Thomas Eldridge's uncommonly successful tavern business began when he was just twenty-one years old with the purchase of the Friendly Tavern, just across the street from what would soon become Tom's Tavern. His secondary role at the Friendly was as its bouncer, something he may not have been particularly well suited for, as he only stood at a rather unimposing five feet, ten inches (and wore thick glasses, making confrontations rather difficult).

Even before he arrived in Boulder, Eldridge was already the primary earner in his household. A Chicago native born in 1938, Eldridge lost his father in 1945; Tom, his mother and his sisters moved to Denver five years later. As an adolescent, young Tom had an unruly, troublesome nature, and so his grandfather shipped him off to Marmion Academy, a military institution back in Illinois. Thus "straightened out," Eldridge cooked for Illinois Railroad crews, took classes at CU Boulder and finally purchased the Friendly Tavern in 1959. He opened Tom's Tavern in 1962 and quickly became "Boulder's Burger Baron," famous for his delicious, slow-cooked and never frozen burgers accompanied by thick-cut fries. The atmosphere was comfortable and amiable, welcoming and friendly to any hungry college student, businessman or family stopping in for lunch. Eldridge could often be found working hard in an office above the restaurant, but just as often, he would mingle with his staff, flipping burgers or running food if the tavern was busy.

Eldridge wore a number of hats outside the tavern. He was an avid scuba diver, a compassionate landlord, a dedicated father and husband and a rather renowned member of the city council. Tom had a reputation for being business-oriented within the council, but he also pushed hard for issues related to climate change or environmental action, as well as affordable housing. One of his tenants remembers a visit from Tom rather fondly. In the 1980s, Eldridge swung by in a routine visit to tell each tenant his plans to raise the rent, and he did so simply: "I'm raising the rent." This particular tenant was married, and his wife was pregnant. She walked into the room to join the conversation just as Tom had uttered this sentence, and as soon as he saw her, he followed it with another: "I'm not going to raise the rent." He understood the needs of individuals as well as families, and he had a reputation among all who knew him as being concise as well as disarmingly compassionate.

In 1967, Eldridge formulated his famous tavern burger, a generous half-pounder with a side of fries that cost eighty-five cents. The price would rise slowly over the years, topping out at seven dollars in 2007, the year Tom died of brain cancer. He bequeathed the restaurant to Daniel, the eldest of his four children, who wanted to keep the tavern in the family. However, everyone knew that the real Tom's died with Tom, and the tavern closed shortly after Daniel took it over. Daniel has been quoted as saying that he never was all that interested in personally running his father's business, which is understandable—growing up in the tavern must make a change of scenery rather appealing. Most of Tom's regulars agreed that it was better that way, that the real secret to Tom's burgers and ambiance was just, well, Tom.

The empty building was not vacant for long. The corner of Eleventh and Pearl, the west edge of the mall, has always been well traveled, and the real estate was appetizing to many a restaurateur. The area was already home to many of Boulder's most popular gastronomic experiments, such as the Kitchen and Centro, not to mention the well-known staples of Pasta Jay's and Trident Café. So it came as no surprise when Bradford Heap, the man behind the wildly successful restaurant Colterra, scooped up the property and began planning a new farm-to-table concept. Thus, in 2009, Salt was born.

Salt Bistro has taken little bits of both Tom's and Trezise Undertaking and created a richly textured old-town ambiance. Carol Vilate, Heap's wife and partner, made sure that as many materials as possible were salvaged. Floor joists more than one hundred years old were used to re-create the original mortuary door, Tom's old booths were reupholstered for a trendier seating option and the building's original tin ceiling was revealed and allowed to shine for the first time in decades. With each nod to the past, the owners of the bistro have worked a rich sense of history into its experience—the old Tom's Tavern mural, for example, still bedecks the Eleventh Street side of the façade. Even more touching than the physical respect for the past, however, is Salt's reverence for the spirits that have passed through the space.

Carol Vilate is a tough woman to get in touch with—she stays busy year-round within the restaurant business, so a few days of phone tag are to be expected. Her responses to questions of a paranormal nature, however, were both playful and informative. Straightforward as always, Carol provided us with a pretty clear picture of what was to be found at Salt from the day she and Heap took over the lease.

"No one went downstairs, after it was a mortuary," she began. "It was mostly used for storage, and the floor was dirt." Vilate detailed how she and the barrage of local artists and friends that enlisted to help create Salt went down into that storage space, sifted through the earth and found things—old things. She remembered that, as they were down in the dirt, she and her "miners," as she affectionately labeled her helpers, felt crowded, as though there was simply not enough space. "There just wasn't enough room, like there was a bunch of energy in the way." Respectful of the dead, Vilate did what any number of rational people looking to operate a business in a "crowded" space might do: she held psychic cleansings.

Before the cleansings, there were reports of shadows seen in the periphery when friends and employees were working late—people flitting about the corners of their vision. Were they the spirits of the mortuary workers or of their clients? Carol and her friends centered their cleansings around the stairs down to the embalming room, the same stairs that Trezise and his crew used to carry bodies down and back up again in preparation for burial. They set up a little altar with crystals and candles, they played drums and sang and they offered the spirits options as far as where to go—into the crystals or on to the next world. If they chose to stay, Carol bargained, they were asked respectfully to behave.

After the first few months, unofficially, the bartenders were instructed to keep a full place setting at the bar for the spirits who remained and for them only—no one else was to sit there, nor was the setting to be cleared. For the most part, Salt has been relatively quiet ever since. Vilate reports that it is not uncommon for her female employees to visit the wine cellar only in pairs after having ventured alone once or twice—they saw shadows or, at the very least, didn't feel alone, and that was enough for a few to request a buddy on their next wine run.

After the interview reached its conclusion, Vilate was sure to emphasize one thing in particular: "We *love* this building—couldn't be happier." Despite the building's long and somewhat gruesome history as a mortuary, its denizens and visitors alike find themselves in a warm and inviting space, much livelier than it was more than a century ago.

On a lovely afternoon in the spring of 2013, Krista Socash was kind enough to meet us for refreshments at Salt's Mermaid Bar. We had corresponded about the possibility of getting a reading of the restaurant, and she agreed to "see what happened." Upon our arrival, we had a seat at the bar, and Krista excused herself to the restroom. When she came back, she sat down and said, "Well, the young woman in the restroom is interesting!" She described the spirit of a young woman who seems to be grieving and who called out to Krista when she entered. Surprisingly, the spirit felt very similar to the same spirit that Krista feels every time she visits the Hotel Boulderado—that Boulderado spirit resides in the main-floor restroom in the hotel lobby as well. A mischievous male spirit showed himself as well; he isn't a permanent resident of the old mortuary, but he does like to knock a bottle over now and then. Overall, Krista thought that the place was very quiet and that it just "felt good" to her.

Psychic Krista Socash gets in touch with the spirits at Salt Bistro. *Photo by Ann Alexander Leggett.*

Our conversation wasn't over, however. As it turned out, there used to be a ballet studio above the restaurant, and Krista danced there for upward of ten years. She clearly remembered that after about 4:00 p.m. each day, the students would bolt down the long stairway after class because no one could stand to stay there any later. They all felt apprehensive and uncomfortable in the early evening. Today, it seems that things have quieted down a good deal, and we left Salty hour satisfied—as did our curiosity.

So go visit on a warm summer day and see if it is just a little more crowded than it appears to be, catch that cool breeze emanating from the basement and sit in plain sight of the end of the bar. You may see a guest you didn't expect, dressed in a canvas apron and sleeves, doffing his cap as he heads down to the basement for one last day of work.

THE ORIGINAL HAUNTED HOUSE

Ask Boulder's older citizens, those who grew up here in the early 1900s, and they'll all tell you the same thing: the Harbeck House is the city's original haunted house. Stories of strange lights and ghostly figures in the windows were the fodder for what became a self-perpetuating urban legend of sorts. Everyone knew that the house must be haunted...after all, it's the Harbeck House.

Sitting at the corner of Twelfth and Euclid, the house is a grand sight indeed. Built in 1899 by J.H. Harbeck as a summer home, the house was known for its unique architectural style and, for a time, was probably the most imposing home in town. Three stories tall and faced with Indiana limestone, its oversized cornice, Grecian Ionic columns and a nine-foot-high Tiffany stained-glass window add to its eclectic charm. Harbeck and his wife, Katherine, lived in New York City, where he worked as a stockbroker and owned a thriving dry goods chain. Having made his fortune in the shipping industry, historical records report that Harbeck also owned the glorious Plaza Hotel.

Summering in Colorado proved to be beneficial to John's health, and although they socialized with a small group of friends when visiting, they remained somewhat to themselves. This is where some of the strange tales of the Harbeck House originate.

Kate's fear of illness prompted her to appear in public with her face covered, often wearing a dark veil. The Harbecks traveled about town in an elaborate carriage with the curtains drawn. The couple's love of their three

The Harbeck House, shown here in the early 1900s, is known by many locals as Boulder's "original haunted house." *Carnegie Branch Library for Local History, Boulder Historical Society Collection.*

dogs—Jim, Rover and Beauty—would become a legend of its own. As the Harbecks were childless, the dogs became their "children" and were regarded as members of the family. As time passed and the dogs died, they were each grieved and honored with expensive funerals, complete with caskets, hearses and headstones. The dogs were buried in a plot in Katherine's garden on the southwest side of the home.

John died in 1910 in New York City, leaving Katherine with the Boulder home. His will is said to have stipulated that the house, all its furnishings and the dogs' graves remain undisturbed for a period of twenty-two years.

Honoring her husband's wishes, and still grieving for her "two boys" and her "girl" herself, Kate arranged to hire a caretaker to watch over the empty house and care for the graves. According to DeAnne Butterfield, executive director of the Boulder History Museum, the caretaker, Charles McAllister, apparently had a vivid imagination and told local children ghost stories to keep them at bay while the house remained unoccupied. But the stories took on a life of their own, with rumors of occult activities and flickering lights in the windows—lights that may have been lit by old Charlie himself simply to ward off would-be burglars. The local children believed that the sober gray house was haunted, however, and could not be convinced otherwise. Those children, now grown old and with children of their own, still believe it is haunted.

For years, the house and the dogs' graves stood undisturbed. Kate Harbeck died in 1931 when she was tragically crushed in a revolving door at the Plaza Hotel, her New York City home. Since the death of her husband more than twenty years earlier, she had never returned to Colorado, and the dining room table in her Boulder home was still set for a dinner party that was never held.

In 1929, the University of Colorado, faced with rapidly increasing enrollment, briefly considered purchasing the mansion for use as a girls' dormitory. Whether due to its haunted reputation or for other reasons, the sale of the property apparently fell through. The Harbeck House stood isolated and empty for nearly thirty years before it became home to different families over several years. In 1937, the land surrounding the house was purchased by William Beach and became what is now known as Beach Park.

Kate Harbeck died a very wealthy woman, and her generous will bequeathed $50,000 to the Society for the Prevention of Cruelty to Animals, a local chapter of which eventually became the Boulder Humane Society. It was her wish that the remains of her cherished dogs be reinterred at a pet cemetery, located at the time in a field on Arapahoe Avenue. Her wishes were honored, and it is believed that the dogs' remains are still buried in that property's tall grass, well away from the bustling city life that surrounds them now.

The Bergheim family lived in the house for thirty years, first appearing as residents of the grand house at 1260 Euclid on the 1940 census. Milton Bergheim owned and operated a popular clothing store on Pearl Street in bustling downtown Boulder. The three Bergheim children—two boys and a girl—were a lively bunch and, with the help of their young mother, Violet, turned one of the upstairs rooms into a roller-skating rink. Milton Jr, Joe and little Marjorie must have brought the same life to the old gray house as the Harbeck's "children" once did. The house became a place of activity and family gatherings, quite a change from its lonely interim of drawn curtains and locked doors.

Since becoming the home of the Boulder History Museum in 1985, the ghost stories surrounding the Harbeck House have slowly faded away. Now the museum is set to reopen in 2014 in another supposedly haunted location, the Boulder Masonic Lodge building at 2205 Broadway, next to the Carnegie Branch Library. But maybe we shouldn't be so quick to dismiss the ghostly activity even though stories about the house have waned. While visiting the house a few years ago, psychic Brian Hall felt the presence of a woman watching over the home. "I sensed that this was her house, and she was very protective of it," he says. "She is still there watching over it and guarding it." Hall felt her spirit standing at the window of what was once a bedroom on the top floor looking out over the garden.

Perhaps the protective spirits of Katherine's faithful dogs still patrol the grounds. Do other ghosts still roam the halls of the Harbeck House? Ask around. You'll be surprised at what you hear.

THE HOTEL BOULDERADO

You can check out any time you like, but you can never leave.
—the Eagles, "Hotel California"

On New Year's Eve, the residents of Boulder brave the subfreezing temperatures and flock downtown. They dress in their finest and flashiest, wandering from Pearl Street to Walnut to Canyon and stopping at various bars and parties on the way. A good majority of the throng will have passed through or ended their evening at the Catacombs beneath the famed Hotel Boulderado, home of the New Year's Eve Gala Ball. This decadent ringing-in of the New Year is a tradition that has been perpetuated since the hotel's opening on New Year's Eve 1909. One may leave the party for a moment, step out on the sidewalk in the crisp night air and drink in the grandeur of an aged Boulder landmark—the Hotel Boulderado is one of Boulder's most distinctive, standing tall and stately on the corner of Thirteenth and Spruce.

Despite the variable nature of economics in the town surrounding, the Boulderado has weathered many financial downturns fairly well. Once Boulder's ritziest rooms-for-rent, the hotel sheltered citizens both down on their luck and homeless during the 1930s before rising again out of the dust and enjoying a restoration of its original impressive fixtures. The hotel opened with a 1908 Otis elevator within its walls, and that very elevator still runs today, albeit manually, staffed by an operator at all times. The cantilevered cherry staircase has been revitalized along with the famed stained-glass ceiling that caps the dramatic two-story lobby.

The hotel now houses not one but three dining establishments: Q's, an ever-popular fine dining experience; the Corner Bar, offering a more casual option; and the Catacombs, an exceptionally lively component of Boulder's nightlife. Nestled underneath the hotel proper, the Catacombs is rumored to have been the first legal drinking establishment in Boulder after Prohibition was repealed in 1933. The hotel rents rooms as simple as a single with a queen bed or as extravagant as the Presidential Suite, and prices range from $250 to just over $400 a night. Much of the furniture is antique, and the wallpaper and tile floors remind one of another era—one of ballroom dancing and stronger cocktails. The Boulderado is beautiful, but as with all landmarks, its real beauty lies in the history.

In 1905, Boulder was a burgeoning city possessed of the University of Colorado, some eight thousand residents and a grand total of twenty-six automobiles—a 1904 city ordinance had made it "unlawful for any person to ride or drive within Boulder at a rate of speed in excess of six miles per hour." There were rooms to be had for the casual traveler, to be sure, but an influential and forward-thinking group, Boulder's Commercial Association (predecessor to the Boulder Chamber of Commerce), took it upon itself to launch the "hotel proposition" to ensure that Boulder kept growing. The members sold stock in the plan at $100 per share, the Boulder Hotel Company was formed and the idea for a grand and memorable Boulder hotel was born.

Initially, the idea went off without a hitch—Boulder, after all, was a new railroad hub and had seen an increased number of travelers in recent years. The hotel was approved across the board in all respects but one—what it was to be called. A select few voted for its moniker to hint at the president of the Commercial Association, the band of citizens behind the Boulder Hotel Company, while others called for a name honoring Andrew J. Macky of First National Bank fame. Still more dismissed either option and waited for a new solution, one that came from within the Commercial Association itself—the Hotel Boulderado.

As a combination of "Boulder" and "Colorado," the name speaks to the hotel's origin and was defended fiercely by the president of the Commercial Association. Not everyone was sold on the idea, however. L.C. Paddock, editor of Boulder's newspaper the *Daily Camera*, denounced the name on the front page, calling it "an offense against the English language and a rhetorical monstrosity." The president shot back, "It will be the only hotel of that name in all the world…It stands for the city of

The popular Hotel Boulderado as it looked in 1929. *Carnegie Branch Library for Local History, Boulder Historical Society Collection.*

Boulder in the state of Colorado. No matter when or where the words Hotel Boulderado may be heard by anyone who has ever rested beneath its roof…not Boulder in Montana, nor Boulder in Illinois, but Boulder in Colorado will instantly come to his mind whether it be one or twenty years after. And when he thinks of Boulder, he will remember the hotel… he will remember its name." Arguably, the president was right—guests and visitors have found themselves remembering the Boulderado, though perhaps not just for the name alone.

Some of the more famous features within the hotel—the lobby ceiling, the restaurants, the stairs—have their own stories to tell. The lobby's stained glass was originally an homage to the Palace Hotel in San Francisco, whose glass-canopied lobby had set a precedent for opulence in the hospitality industry. On April 18, 1906, 80 percent of San Francisco was destroyed by the Great San Francisco Earthquake, and the Palace Hotel numbered just one of its casualties. The Hotel Boulderado, still in the planning stages, adopted the Palace's design on a smaller scale, even down to the import of cathedral glass from Italy. In 1959, unfortunately, a heavier-than-usual snowfall knocked out a skylight, destroying a section of the stained glass. The whole ceiling was replaced by patriotic red, white and blue Plexiglas. By 1977, however, the beautiful stained glass was back—a new design restored the lobby's original turn-of-the-century ambiance—and in 2004, an extensive remodel and restoration of the ceiling was accomplished. Other lobby features include the hotel's original safe, a white marble water fountain that recalls a time when Boulder's water supply was direct from the Arapahoe Glacier and the original, century-old mosaic tile floor.

The cherry staircase is a mystery, according to Beverly Silva, the hotel's director of sales and marketing. She began work at the Boulderado in 1983 as a housekeeper, working her way through her bachelor's degree at the University of Colorado. Her postgrad dreams of building plans and architecture firms gave way to a comfortable sense of belonging within the hotel, and she quickly climbed the ranks of management. Her experiences in the hotel are many and varied, but she mentioned in an interview that even hotel historians have very little idea of the origin of the cherry wood panels that make up the six-story staircase. "No one knows how it got here," said Silva. Wherever it came from, it is one of the most popular spots for photos in the city, with the balcony overlooking the lobby ideal for wedding proposals and even ceremonies.

Eating is a large part of any vacation—what's the point of staying somewhere luxurious if the food doesn't match? For anyone from the casual diner to the guest of honor, the Hotel Boulderado has managed to provide a dining experience to rival its rich history. Q's, perhaps the most famous of the three establishments within the Boulderado, is the more formal and is located on the right side of the main entrance off Thirteenth Street. It began its life as the formal dining room but transitioned through phases as varied as a 1950s coffee shop, a Winston's Seafood Restaurant in the '80s and the Theodore Roosevelt Grill (affectionately known as "Teddy's," named for the Boulderado's famous guest himself) in the '90s before coming to life as Q's. Chef John Platt and his wife, Sabrina, purchased the restaurant space from David Query in 1993, and they have since made Q's one of the top fine-dining restaurants in Boulder. In keeping with the city's progressive reputation, the theme is "sustainable, local, organic," winning the restaurant several awards in its two decades of operation.

For guests and locals looking for a quicker, more casual bite, the Corner Bar is an offshoot of Q's. It is home to one of the best happy hours in Boulder and operates with the same attention to detail as Q's without the necessity of calling ahead. The Bar sits inside one of two repurposed storefronts that graced Thirteenth Street until 1963—storefronts that used to house clothing boutiques, barbershops and, once upon a time, the chamber of commerce.

Finally, underneath it all lies the Catacombs, one of the hottest bars in the downtown area. Although the name isn't exactly accurate—there are no actual catacombs beneath the building—the implications are present in the many tales surrounding the hotel. Almost every guest, it seems, has some idea of just how haunted the Boulderado is.

The web of stories about this hotel is vast and tangled. A simple Google search for "Haunted Hotel Boulderado" yields page after page of rumors, testimonials and flippant reviews. Suites 302 and 304, adjoining, are the focal point of many of the tales—to the point that a guest once refused to enter one room because there was "something supernatural" within and abruptly quit the hotel at 2:00 a.m.—and certainly, there is a decent amount of history behind most. Some tales, including those of disembodied voices, full-body apparitions and flickering electronics, remain unattached to the "legitimate" history of the hotel but are speculatively tied to rumor. As with many popular sites of paranormal activity, the more lurid of the tales have taken this hotel's history and run with it.

One fine summer night in 2003, a retired British policeman and his wife inhabited a room on the fifth floor. They had been staying there for about a week while looking for a home to buy to aid in their permanent move from England to Boulder. After a long day of searching and visiting open houses, they retired, only to be awoken in the wee hours by the sound of footsteps in the hall. Characterized as "a slow stagger or limp," the steps awakened a need for investigation in the ex-officer, and he flung open the door. He found nothing and no one in the empty hallway. Upon relaying the story to the elevator operator, the couple was regaled with the story of a bride who, left at the altar by her fiancé, threw herself to her death from their very window. Had the British couple heard the fateful steps of a jilted spirit? While there have been a number of documented suicides in the Boulderado, there is no record of such a bride or such a death. There was, however, a wedding party that was disturbed by paranormal events.

Boulder County Paranormal Research Society conducted an investigation at the Hotel Boulderado on October 30, 2007. Richard Estep, the team leader and cofounder of BCPRS, put together a succinct report about the findings that night—which amounted to almost nothing. They did record an electronic voice phenomenon (EVP), a voice that sounded much like the world "careful." Estep received an e-mail not too long after from a woman whose daughter had been recently married at the Boulderado. A recent follower of the society's doings, the woman had read of the investigation on its website. Nancy, the mother of the bride, mentioned that she was glad she didn't come across the BCPRS website until after she and her husband had attended their daughter's wedding.

The family of the bride (her parents, her brother and her sister-in-law) specifically requested the adjoining rooms 302 and 304 for the additional space the wedding party would likely need. The two rooms also share a balcony. Cautious by nature, Nancy and her husband had a pre-bed ritual of double-checking all locks, and they were especially careful to do so while traveling—even the door to the balcony. After the wedding and reception, Nancy and her husband fell into bed, exhausted, but both of them distinctly remembered checking and rechecking every door in their suite.

Just as Nancy was drifting off to sleep, she heard the main door open. The rest of her night went as such:

> *Shocked, I jump out of bed, dash into the other room—door is closed & locked. I check out the rest of the room, nobody there, so back to bed. The rest of the night I hear a squeeky door open & close numerous times, room is cold, movement in the room and an uncomfortable feeling and I finally just pull the covers over my head (something I never do) because I'm so tired and just don't want to see anything. Husband sleeps thru it all.*

In the morning, Nancy relayed the details to her husband. In an effort to arrive at an explanation, they tried to re-create the noises, to no avail. When they returned home, he remembered a spine-tingling tidbit: he had found the balcony door unlocked and open that morning, although it cannot be unlocked from outside. Thoroughly unsettled to this day, Nancy ended her e-mail to us with a cheerful salutation: "Best Wishes (won't be back to the Boulderado), Nancy." The room numbers had been changed during an extensive remodel, but perhaps one of the deaths on record at the hotel took place in those adjoining suites.

A similar story took place just a few years later, in September 2011. A guest and her husband checked in for two nights, and they marveled at the grandeur and the luxurious feel of the hotel. The first night, they had no complaints. On the second, however, they awoke at 3:15 a.m. to a furious and deafening pounding on one wall of their room. They put their hands over the spot that sounded the loudest and felt distinct vibrations—something was striking the other side with considerable force. Frantic, they called the front desk, and the night manager arrived to inspect the room (from the relative safety of the hallway, of course). The sound had ended by that time, and it took the couple more than an hour for the adrenaline to dissipate and allow them to drift back to an unsettled sleep. In the morning, before they checked out, they asked what room was on the other side of that wall, only to learn that there wasn't one—it was an exterior wall, with nothing behind it, and their room was on the third floor. In an e-mail to BCPRS, the woman stated that "[the] place was lovely, the staff friendly, but I was too scared to ever return again."

The first and most famous suicide occurred in 1924. Lou and Mary Ellen Pfeiffer, a middle-aged couple from Denver, took the train into Boulder and booked a room in the hotel. The clerk registered the seemingly innocuous couple and handed over the room key. Arm in arm, the couple retreated upstairs and passed a deceptively quiet evening. What the staff didn't know, however, was that the Pfeiffers had a suicide pact, and they intended to carry out the ending of their lives within the walls of the Boulderado. Lou was unemployed and suffering from kidney trouble that was likely going to prove fatal. Mary Ellen, in love with her husband, allowed herself to be persuaded to follow him in death so they wouldn't be separated. They registered under a fake name and retreated upstairs to utilize the chloroform they had purchased en route from Denver.

Mary Ellen went to calm her nerves with a bath, but when she reentered the bedroom, she found that Lou had preceded her in death after all—he had administered a fatal dose of chloroform whilst she soaked just a few feet away. Mary Ellen lay down next to her husband's still body and self-administered what remained, slipping into unconsciousness shortly thereafter. However, she woke up a few hours later with a pounding headache—there hadn't been enough chloroform left to kill her. She headed for the nearest pharmacy, placing a note on the door of the room as she left: "Do not disturb: sick man in room." After asking for a full pint of chloroform and receiving only four ounces, Mary Ellen tried again—she didn't succeed that time, either. She awoke again and fled, leaving her belongings and Lou in the room where they had planned to die.

Upon the discovery of Lou's body and the left-behind luggage, authorities soon discerned the Pfeiffers' true identities. They found Mary Ellen in a Denver hospital. She told them, "We were just two unlucky people who had grown tired of living. He was all I had to live for. It was all a mistake, I see clearly now. Instead of sympathizing with him in a desire to end it all, I should have diverted his mind." Charges against Mary Ellen (including aiding and abetting suicide) were dropped, and Lou was buried in Boulder's famed Columbia Cemetery. Perhaps the spirit of poor Lou still roams the hotel, impatiently seeking his sincere but feckless wife. Lou had a rather passive, if unaccompanied death, however, so it can be argued that his is not the spirit that causes guests of the Boulderado to stir in the middle of the night.

Another oft-told story is that of the woman in gray on the stairs. Not limited simply to guests or passersby, staff members and even denizens of surrounding buildings have reported this full-body apparition—even a respected firefighter, employed as a security man across the street. Reports having seen her in the wee hours of the morning. No one knows exactly which historical character she is tied to, but all reports have something in common: she isn't translucent so much as colorless, like an old photograph, and she is seen more than once by the same witnesses.

Juliann, a native Ohioan transplanted to the Denver metropolitan area, tells the story of the woman in gray the best. One summer, she was preparing for a conference taking place at the Boulderado:

> In planning for the conference, I had an initial meeting with a sales and catering director, and the only thing I remember is that her name was Sarah. I went one day to the Boulderado—had been there many times before and knew the property fairly well. From the main lobby I walked up the beautiful staircase to the second floor to meet Sarah. At the turn on the staircase, I passed a woman—or thought I did—and after turning up the second flight of stairs looked back to see her. She wasn't there. What I recall—clearly, and to this day—was that she was dressed very old-fashionedly—a dress that went to the floor, a small hat—and the image was a dark (almost charcoal) gray—no color. Opaque—not transparent or "ghostly" at all…When I met Sarah, I told her what I saw. Her response was one of no surprise—as though she had heard it before.

Juliann passed the rest of the morning as would be expected, touring the hotel and taking notes, all of it very pleasant. Her exit, however, was a little more memorable: "As I walked *down* the staircase, I once again passed a woman. *The same woman.* She was walking up, past me. As I turned to the second flight down, I again looked to see her—and she was gone. I seem to recall that *she made eye contact with me.*" Although she moved back to Ohio soon after, Juliann has never been able to shake the memory of the woman on the stairs and still yearns to revisit the grandeur of the Boulderado.

There were two other suicides by gunshot in the Hotel Boulderado, one even including a note, but one death within its walls goes largely unmentioned. Hugh Mark, an owner and manager of the hotel in the early twentieth century, had a heart attack mid-meal in the dining room. Mark came onto the staff as assistant manager in 1912, when William Beattie bought the hotel. He took over as manager in 1917, just one year after the birth of his son, Bill, and a few short months after the first concrete sidewalks were poured on Pearl Street. Helen Keller came to speak at Macky Auditorium at the University of Colorado in 1923, and she stayed in the Hotel Boulderado, adding her name to the long list of famous guests that includes Robert Frost and Clarence Darrow, within Mark's lifetime alone. Mark died at breakfast on July 3, 1934, and Boulder mourned the passing of "the biggest little man" in town.

For someone who lived the majority of his adult life, had children and devoted his sweat, blood and tears to the hotel, Hugh Mark doesn't seem to make his presence known. Or if he does, it may be that he is behind some of the more anonymous hauntings. Beverley Silva recalls a ponderously heavy window in Q's dining room opening more than halfway on its own one day. C.M. Johnson of the front desk fought a window one day; she struggled and failed to open it and left to get a tool. Upon her return, it was wide open. She closed it, left and found it open again when she walked past a few minutes later. The elevator also has a mind of its own, stopping on empty floors when no one is there to push buttons. Guests frequently report unaccountable footsteps, scratching in the walls and various voices calling in the night.

In keeping with the rich atmosphere of the grand old hotel, patrons have often reported a woman in a long Victorian gown and shawl rocking in her chair all night or occasionally sitting on the end of an occupied bed in the wee hours of the morning. Despite all of this, guests continue to flock to the hotel during every season, believers and skeptics alike.

Even members of the staff have grown accustomed to the happenings, agreeing that of all hotels, this one would be a rather nice place to haunt. Silva remarked with a chuckle, "I'm going to be a ghost here someday." Perhaps she will, joining the ranks of the many ghostly denizens that reside within the venerable brick walls of the Hotel Boulderado.

HAUNTINGS ON PINE

In July 1996, when the Middletons moved into their home on Pine Street with their young family in tow, they had no idea that they would be sharing the house with its resident spirits. As they went about settling into their two-story, foursquare-style home, there were no obvious signs that there were spirits about. But Kathryn Middleton immediately had a feeling, a definite sense that there was more to the house than they realized.

It was about two to three months later that the flickering of the master bedroom light fixture began at about the same time every night. Kathryn remembers the approximate time of day the flickers started and how she would try to tie them in with the heater coming on—or the dishwasher, or any other household appliances that might make the energy fluctuate. It was an old house, after all. Although the pattern seemed to repeat itself each evening like clockwork, it did not coincide with the refrigerator or other appliances activating. Only the light in the master bedroom was affected, and the flickers persisted.

The home was built in 1904, and the Middletons were the ninth owners when they purchased the quaint little house. According to records from Boulder's Carnegie Branch Library, the house was built by James Park and his wife, Mary B. Park. Mr. Park was a local banker who retired in 1910, and a historic building inventory report notes that he died in California in 1947. Kathryn had a clear idea of who her resident ghost was when the hauntings started. "I just had a feeling it was the woman who lived in the home from the late 1940s through 1989. When we moved in, I also heard

Some private residences in the city have the best haunting stories. *Photo by Ann Alexander Leggett.*

from neighbors that a woman had convalesced in what is now the dining room, but I didn't have any more details."

The hauntings began to increase, and Kathryn began to feel some activity on the stairs to the second floor. "I always felt as though there was someone on the stairs behind me, and when I'd go down to get the baby a bottle, I'd even run back up the stairs because it felt kind of creepy." Then, one day, she saw the image of a woman in a red robe on the landing of the stairway, and her suspicions were confirmed.

Her husband, James, who up until that point had been somewhat skeptical, corroborated the sense of energy on the stairway. One night, while carrying his then two-year-old son up the stairs, they encountered an area of freezing cold air on the first landing. "Ghost, daddy," the boy said. They both shivered because of the sudden cold and looked up to see the filmy image of a woman standing before them. The woman appeared to be older and was dressed in white. James particularly remembers her high-collared white blouse. The image then disappeared. He was now a believer in the ghost his wife had been describing. The little boy, on the other hand, seems to have accepted the spirit's presence in the home from the very beginning.

During the summer of 2000, the Middletons were knee-deep in a major remodeling of the home and actually moved out so the construction could be completed. Wallpaper was stripped, walls were moved and bathrooms were redone. The renovation was quite extensive.

One morning, Kathryn came by the home with her two sons and stood outside on the front sidewalk, watching them play, before she entered to talk with the workmen. "I felt the strangest sensation that someone was watching me from my front window," she said. Slowly, she turned and faced the house. In the bottom-right corner of the front picture window was the face of a woman. "She was wearing a white, high-collared blouse, and her hair was pulled back severely. Obviously, I was startled, and I got the immediate impression that she was angry with me for remodeling the house. That was what she looked like."

Thinking that someone might have entered the home during the construction, Kathryn gathered the children and went upstairs to one of the bedrooms, where a workman was working behind a door. "Seen any ghosts today?" she asked him jokingly. The man put down his tools and looked up at her in disbelief. "Funny you should say that," he said. "I've had the strangest sensation that someone has been in this room deliberately closing this door all morning. Every time I opened it, it closed. I was getting ready to take it off its hinges and rehang it."

With the construction completed, the family moved back into the home, and the ghost activity resumed. On one particularly late night, after spending a long day preparing for her son's birthday party, Kathryn was walking down the hallway with a light bulb in her hand when a force sent it shattering against the wall. "I could feel the force as though someone had deliberately knocked it right out of my hand," she said. "That has been the only incident of the ghost being mean." By this time, Kathryn was familiar with the ghost, but this incident startled her because it was out of character. Too tired, she cleaned up the mess and went to bed.

Yet another indication of resident spirits was evident in the living room, where from time to time an obnoxious odor—a cross between sulfur and dead fish—could be detected in the corner. The Middletons assumed that the offensive smell was in the old carpeting, but cleaning did nothing to remove it. Kathryn said that during the remodel, the carpet had been torn out of the room, a logical recourse that should have all but ensured that the smell would vanish. She was wrong. While it wasn't noticed again for some time, the smell returned and lingered long after the remodeling.

Psychic Krista Socash did an interpretation of the spirits in the home and was able to verify a great deal of what the Middletons had been experiencing. "It seems like the woman on the stairs is waiting for someone, perhaps a suitor," Krista said. "She seems to be thinking about a decision she has made about marriage. She left the home at an early age and has come back after her death." In addition to a woman on the stairs, however, Krista felt the strong presence of a young girl near the small bedroom at the top of the stairs.

The spirit of the young girl near the little bedroom was of particular interest to Kathryn. A large closet before the renovations, the space was enlarged and transformed into a nursery for her eighteen-month-old daughter. Krista sensed that the young spirit loved little children and that she had a very playful presence. "I have often felt that the energy in my daughter's room was so different from that in the rest of the house," Kathryn said. "It has always seemed so feminine and very nurturing." Initially, she had her son sleeping in the room, but he never slept well. Kathryn moved him to another bedroom and redecorated the small space for her daughter. It seemed to have been the right choice. On several occasions, she was surprised when her daughter appeared to be playing with someone in her crib and didn't want to be taken out. As Kathryn left her daughter's room at bedtime one evening, she suddenly felt a rush of very cold air at her feet. "I knew it was the spirit going into my daughter's room. I just said, 'Okay, leave her alone now, it's her bedtime,' and the air vanished."

Throughout the months of new homeownership and remodeling, Kathryn and her family had sensed ghost activity in the lower level of the home, on the stairway and sometimes in her daughter's room. Whereas their experiences seemed to be limited to those few areas, Krista, in her psychic assessment, found spirit energies of differing natures throughout the house. During her visit, she felt the presence of a bitter, angry, older woman downstairs in the dining room area, very different from the playful spirit upstairs. Was this the severe woman Katherine saw peering through the window during the remodel? Krista suggested that while spirits are not typically angry about renovations, they do feel "lost" because of the changes made to the home. Kathryn spoke with a ninety-year-old neighbor, a retired physician who vividly remembered making house calls to the Pine Street home in the 1950s. According to the physician, one female resident of the home was very sullen and seemed unhappy, perhaps due to the fact that she was asthmatic and had been housebound for many years.

Krista also felt the spirit of an older man in the living room, specifically in the northeast corner. A framed picture had been hung on the wall above where his spirit sat, and according to Kathryn, the picture was crooked every day, even after repeated efforts to straighten it. "He's playing with you," Krista told Kathryn. "He's making himself known." Krista had the sense that this particular spirit was reproachful and upset. "He is someone's father, and he's disapproving of his family's lifestyle. He is also irritated by a female presence in the house." Krista tied the odor in the living room directly to the male spirit.

The hallway that extended from the front entrance of the home to the bright, cheerful kitchen was another hot spot for Krista. "The energy there is very heavy and dark," she said. Kathryn spoke of having the urge to run the length of the hall to reach the safety of the kitchen. Interestingly, although Kathryn's husband had constructed a small office nook off the hallway, he grew to experience discomfort and uneasiness if he spent any amount of time there. According to Krista, this is very understandable. She sensed that a fight had occurred in the hallway outside the office and that the spirit of a sick little boy was present. Her advice? Move the office to the cellar.

In contrast, the cellar had a fun, almost jovial atmosphere, very different from the rest of the house. It had become a storage room of sorts, as most cellars do, and James soon felt at home there in his relocated office. Whenever the Middletons had a party, all the men seemed to congregate in the cellar, also not surprising to Krista. She immediately sensed a male spirit in the cellar, a spirit that enjoyed fun and games. Kathryn had tried to put her sewing room down there, but it just didn't feel right. The cellar belonged to the men.

Even with their resident spirits, the Middletons enjoyed their home. "This is the type of house I have always dreamed of," Kathryn said. "I will live here forever. I enjoy the spirits in my home." With Kathryn's sympathetic disposition, it's obvious that the old house on Pine came to be in good hands. With minds and hearts open to the spirits of the past, a family who lives with spirits may discover even more secrets within their homes.

Author's note: I worked on setting up meetings with Kathryn and Krista for about a two-week period. During that time, I was also doing historical research on the home. Concrete details were hard to come by, and initially I was stuck with only basic information, including the fact that the home was built in 1904. I had a sheet of paper with the information about the house next to my computer. After we met at the home, I was surprised to get a call from a friend, who wondered why in the world my e-mails were coming to her with such strange dates. I immediately went to my "send" file and found that all of the e-mails I had been sending out during that two-week period had gone out with the wrong date. I checked my desktop setup to determine the source of the problem. Sure enough, the date on the computer somehow had been set to 1904.—A.A.L.

THE KOHLER HOUSE

Tucked tidily into a well-foliaged lot not four blocks from the famed Hotel Boulderado lies 942 Pine Street, more formally known as the Kohler House. Almost four thousand square feet, the house was built in 1903 by Frederick Kohler for his family. It stayed within the Kohler family until 1943 and remained a single-family home until 1965, when it was converted into apartments. The seven-bedroom house has been owned by Boulder landlord Catherine Schweiger since 1976, and she has been responsible for its upkeep as several sets of tenants have moved into and out of it. In its 110 years of "life," the house has seen at least three deaths—and a few more funerals besides—although none since the conversion to apartment-style living. Throughout its tenure as a residence, there have been many first- and secondhand accounts of hauntings that stem from the history of the house—cats snuggling up to spirits, dogs barking at empty rooms—but let us begin with Frederick Kohler himself.

Kohler was born in Saxony, Germany, in the fall of 1832. His father held an esteemed public office comparable to an American justice of the peace, and Kohler was one of eight children who lived and grew on the German Kohler homestead. As a young man of eighteen, Kohler arrived in New York City and traveled to work on a farm in Pennsylvania. He began humbly as an immigrant, making only $100 per year, a relatively modest sum even in the 1850s. Over the course of seven years, he both gained a working knowledge of English and elevated himself to a salary of $14 per month, more than one and a half times his starting pay. By the end of his stint in Pennsylvania, he had saved up $600, a sum he used to travel to the mountains of Calaveras County, California.

He had caught the tail end of gold fever, it seems, and settled down to prospect in 1856. He placed his small fortune in a bank only to have that bank fold some time after his arrival, leaving him almost destitute. The bank was called the Adams Express Bank and was supposedly attached to the well-established Adams Express Company. Kohler, along with many other prospectors, awoke one morning to find that the bank sign had been removed and that the owners had disappeared with their hard-earned wages; Kohler lost a grand total of $1,800. While lesser men might have given up at that point, Kohler redoubled his efforts in the mining business and amassed an even larger fortune than before. In 1862, he left Calaveras County and traveled east until he stopped in Boulder, Colorado.

As a young man just settling in Boulder, Kohler did exceedingly well—after a little trial and error, that is. He originally purchased $800 worth of land but lost it after an assessment found that the sale misrepresented. Undaunted, Kohler acquired a claim on 160 acres, most likely through the Homestead Act, beneath what are now the Table Mesa and Highland Park subdivisions. Over time, he built his holdings up to almost 800 acres of stable and fertile cropland. He continued to invest, particularly in a failed mining venture in Gold Hill, and eventually found himself a stockholder and director of Boulder National Bank.

Maturing into a prominent citizen, Kohler had his fingers in many of Boulder's pies, both political and fraternal. An advocate for education, he served on the school board for two decades, and he was elected Boulder County commissioner twice. He reached the highest level of Masonry and was also affiliated with many of Boulder's other fraternal organizations, including the Elks. This level of community involvement did not keep him from devoting just as much of his life to his family, however. On June 4, 1868, Kohler married Rosetta Viele, the woman with whom he would spend the rest of his life.

Rosetta Viele was of the illustrious family for whom Viele Lake is named. Her parents, James B. Viele and his wife, Lucinda, arrived in Boulder in 1865, bringing with them the first steam-threshing machine in the county. They offered threshing services to farmers in the area and steadily built up Boulder's agricultural community. The Vieles began building their ranch structures out of stone they found on their property, near what is now the corner of Cherryvale and South Boulder Road. As the frontrunners in the agricultural side of Boulder, they eschewed the mining operations that other businessmen found so promising and focused on raising cattle for dairy and

The Kohler House has great history and a few good ghost stories as well. *Photo by Ann Alexander Leggett.*

beef. They soon found themselves supplying the better part of Boulder with Viele-brand dairy products, especially butter.

Rosetta, one of seven Viele children, was soon recognized across the county as being a good match for any bachelor in possession of a good fortune, attached as she was to the well-endowed Viele family. So it comes as little surprise that, six years after his arrival in Boulder and during his growth period as a man of status, thirty-five-year-old Kohler took nineteen-year-old Rosetta as his wife, effectively tying two influential Boulder families together forever.

The Kohlers had three children: Effie first, born in 1869 and dead before her first birthday, followed in 1871 by Frederick Jr. and in 1878 by Charles Edward, affectionately known as "C.E." or just "Ed." As the oldest son, Frederick Jr. found himself following in his father's financial footsteps, working as a cashier at the Boulder National Bank and eventually heading up a new mining company that worked several claims in and around Boulder. Ed, however, embodied his father's other half, the one that loved agriculture and business, and in time, he ended up taking over his father's interests. On June 4, 1901—the thirty-third wedding anniversary of his parents—Ed married Rose Clarissa Carner, and they moved in with Frederick Sr. and Rosetta on the family ranch. After two years, the Kohlers decided that a change of scenery was in order and moved downtown. Frederick Jr. built a home at 943 Spruce, and Frederick Sr. built 942 Pine, where he lived in peace with his wife until his death in 1904.

Despite his peaceful home life, in the fall of 1904, the elder Kohler found himself unable to sleep. He suffered from insomnia for almost three weeks, and he couldn't for the life of him figure out why. Some of his crops were not as large as he had expected, and a few had failed, but he wrote these off as "trifles." Kohler summoned Dr. Dodge to his house on the morning of October 13 and told him the following: "I have nothing I should worry about, and yet I worry. I can't sleep. I have a lot of property; a big income; own considerable bank stock; have money idle in the bank; and my family relations are of the best. I ought to be perfectly contented and not worry, and yet I worry." After the doctor left, Kohler talked to his wife about going to see the farm. He decided, in the end, to stay at home and do some work around the house.

After he had been "around the house" for some time, Rosetta realized that she hadn't seen or heard from him at all since their talk. She asked Frederick Jr. to come to the house, and they searched it room by room. The bathroom door was locked, and no answer was heard in response to their calls and

Fred Kohler took his own life in his house in 1904. *Carnegie Branch Library for Local History, Boulder, Colorado.*

knocks, so Frederick Jr. pried the door open with a crowbar. There, on the floor, they found the lifeless body of Frederick Kohler Sr. According to the newspaper released later that day, Frederick Sr. took "a butcher knife about eight inches long, held aside his heavy whiskers, and with one stroke cut his throat almost from ear to ear." The article went on in grisly detail: "The flesh and the windpipe were cut to the neck bone. The gash was a terrible one. He stood over the bathtub, allowing the blood to run into it as long as his strength held out. Then he fell over to one side and died." After three weeks of incessant worrying and a lack of sleep, Kohler took it upon himself to end his life abruptly and in a fairly violent manner, although he appears to have been concerned about the after-effects of his suicide and thus chose to stand over the tub.

Boulder was scandalized. Frederick Kohler—a wealthy, seemingly happy and affluent businessman—didn't sleep for three weeks and then ended his life in his own house.

Ed and his wife, Rose, moved in with the widowed Rosetta and eventually had four children. Their two daughters lived to adulthood: Margaret Lucille, born in 1906, and Mary Kathryn, born in 1912. Of their sons, Glenn Edward, born in 1902, tragically drowned just shy of his sixteenth birthday. Charles Edward Jr. was born in 1910 but lived only six weeks. Ed, Rose and the first of their children lived with Rosetta until Rosetta's death in 1912, just a few months before Mary Kathryn's birth. Granny Rosie, as she was affectionately known, suffered from cancer and had even gone to the famed Mayo Clinic for treatment. She succumbed to the disease in the house her husband built for her at 2:10 p.m. on February 25, 1912.

After Rosetta's death, the Kohlers remained at 942 Pine. On the Fourth of July 1918, Glenn Edward went swimming at Lakeside, just outside Denver's then city limits. He drowned at the age of fifteen and a half. Mary Kathryn eloped with Raymond Marcus Finch in 1929 at the age of seventeen—she ended up in Sacramento, where she died in 1990, having never seen her childhood home again. Margaret, on the other hand, remained at home and carried on the Kohler household. She was married on her parents' thirty-third wedding anniversary—her grandparents' sixty-sixth—June 4, 1934, in a spectacular garden wedding at her childhood home. Her groom, noted only as having the surname "Floegel," carried her off to California, although she died in North Carolina in 1999.

Ed and Rose continued to live at 942 Pine. Ed lived only nine years after his last child left him—he died of heart failure at the age of sixty-four in his lifelong home. On April 17, 1943, he was found dead in one of the upstairs bedrooms—he had expired at about 2:00 a.m., presumably in his sleep. Rose inherited his entire estate, estimated at $82,500 (just over $1 million in today's economy), the value of both her husband's house and their family ranch near Baseline. A relevant side note: one might assume that Ed's older brother, Frederick Jr., would have inherited his father's estate, but he had preceded Ed in death. In any case, he'd expressed little interest in the ranch or the rest of the Kohler holdings. He'd climbed the ranks and become a successful businessman in his own right—president of Boulder National Bank, no less—and had lived with his wife, Francis, at their house on Spruce until his death, of an abscess from an old ruptured appendix, in 1933.

Shortly after Ed's death, Rose decided to sell the house, taking a smaller apartment and remaining a prominent Boulder clubwoman while still finding time to visit her daughters in California. In the summer of 1969, she was put in Boulder Manor Nursing Home, where she lasted only a few months—she fell, resulting in a fractured hip and a fatal stroke, on September 16.

Up to 1976, the rest of the house's history is essentially hearsay, scrounged from various documents filed with the current owner's application for landmark status. Mildred and Carl G. Anderson purchased the house in 1943. Very little can be found about either of them, although it is speculated that Carl died in the house as well, meaning that every man who had owned this house died in it and left it to his widow. Mildred passed away in 1963, and her children sold the house to a neighbor, Lydia Hochstetter. She and her husband, Reverend J.A Hochstetter, lived at 922 Spruce, just down the road from Frederick Jr.'s old house. Reverend Hochstetter committed suicide in the garage of their house on Spruce shortly before Mildred's death, which left Lydia in need of additional income. After his death, she bought the Kohler House and converted it into apartments, a configuration it has remained in ever since.

Enter Catherine Schweiger, who purchased the house in 1976 for about $92,000—the property is now valued at about $1.2 million—and barring a few remodels, the mansion has remained broken up into Lydia's apartments. Schweiger remembered that upon her purchase, she was warned of a persistent leak in the second-floor bathroom—the site of Frederick Sr.'s demise. She remarked, "Of course, all who knew of the leak said it was his ghost. Being the skeptical sort, I assumed that when I got around to replacing the flooring and having to move the tub to do that job, the leak would stop. It did. It was a good ghost story while it lasted." However, the purported hauntings did not stop with the leak. A longtime tenant, named simply "L." here, reported having experienced the most paranormal activity of any tenant, although a few denizens of the "Main West" apartment—located on the west side of the main floor of the house—have also reported interesting goings-on.

In L.'s years in the Main West apartment, she experienced a rocking chair that rocked all on its own, chimes over the fireplace ringing of their own accord and Christmas ornaments that tinkled on the tree—Schweiger asserted that the apartment is "fairly tight" and that no wind or draft has

The old fireplace in one of the Kohler House apartments seemed spooky to the residents. *Photo courtesy of Kristen Argow.*

been noticed by any of her tenants, so these movements cannot easily be attributed to a crisp Boulder breeze. Another previous tenant, Greg, recalls L. mentioning a few other happenings centered around her fireplace: there were lights in the mantel that could only be turned on or off by screwing or unscrewing the bulbs. L. had gone to bed sometime after unscrewing the bulbs and awoke to them brightly shining, tightly screwed into their sockets. L.'s ancestors were Boulder pioneers, and Greg mentioned that she kept old portraits of them on her mantel; she often found them facedown, as though perhaps Frederick Sr. disapproved of the association. Greg remarked that another tenant walked into a second-floor apartment some ten years ago and saw a full-body apparition—an older, bearded gentleman, fitting the description of Frederick Sr., was standing between the living and dining rooms. He was there just long enough for the tenant to register his appearance, and then he dissipated, leaving no sign of his presence behind.

Another previous Main West tenant, Kristen Argow, lived in the apartment for two and a half years, up until January 2013. Her story takes place in November 2012. Argow had two cats at the time, one diabetic and the other elderly. Her then boyfriend (now husband), Joel, had agreed to stay at her apartment to take care of them while she was out of town attending a conference. He called her on the second night of his stay and told her that he couldn't possibly spend another moment in her apartment. Russ, the diabetic cat, needed two shots a day and more or less constant supervision, so understandably, Argow was upset. As Argow recalled:

> *Joel saw Russ sitting in his favorite chair in the front room, and he thinks someone was holding Russ—a man that was not there. He said he felt the man looking at him, and he felt* [the man] *was upset.* [Joel] *had learned of the history of the house recently, and I told him he was imagining things and needed to stay with my beloved cats. He agreed. Later, he called back and said he had gone home. Russ scratched him out of the blue, and he felt an angry presence in the house telling him to get out—he wouldn't sleep there again. He told me he believed there was a ghost of a man there that liked me and the cats and did not like him.*

While Argow asserted that her husband was letting his imagination get the best of him, this behavior has also been attributed to a disgruntled spirit, likely that of Frederick Kohler Sr. Argow also mentioned that she brought a dog—one that almost never barks—into the apartment, and he stood in the middle of that same front room and barked for quite some time at something no one else could see. She stated that she always felt very safe and happy in the apartment and that if there are any spirits that remain there, she hopes they are those of her cats "being held and loved by the man" that her husband sensed.

Kohler appears to have taken up residence once again at 942 Pine, although whether he is there to stay is as yet undetermined. There have been a multitude of other tenants in the Kohler House throughout the years, and most have reported nothing more than the occasional raccoon strolling about the eaves of a summer evening. What is it that draws this older, bearded gentleman (or young woman, for that matter) to appear to some tenants—or to their pets—and not to others? Whatever it is that attracts the spirits of the Kohlers, perhaps on your next stroll along the Pearl Street Mall, you might take a tangential path through the adjacent neighborhood. See for yourself if there's anything about your person that draws this spirit's fancy. You could soon be the author of your own ghost story.

DEAR OLD CU

Looking at an aerial photograph of Boulder, you're sure to notice the abundance of red tile roofs atop beautiful flagstone buildings, all arranged prettily just shy of the foot of the famed Flatirons. This is the University of Colorado's Boulder campus. Home to thirty thousand undergraduate students from all over the world, CU Boulder has a variety of reputations ranging from "No. 1 Party School" to "Public Ivy." Nobel laureates, astronauts, scientists, researchers and a notoriously dramatic football team all call CU their home. The university is partially responsible for Boulder's success as a city, in a way—it was founded in 1876, just five months before Colorado became a state—and so it only makes sense that this aged and beautiful campus be inhabited by more than just the usual lively college students. Over the years, the rumor mill has churned out some of the juiciest ghost stories around Boulder, and it is only fitting that the university merits a full chapter within this book as a result.

A brief history of CU Boulder is in order. Just before Colorado joined the Union, the territorial legislature made an amendment to the proposed state constitution allowing for funding the establishment of the University of Colorado, the Colorado School of Mines in Golden and Colorado Agricultural College in Fort Collins (now known as Colorado State University, CU's main rival in all things athletic). The university's location wasn't set, and the decision was between Cañon City and Boulder, with the consolation prize—the new state prison—going to the loser. As the debate raged on, Cañon City was at a distinct disadvantage as it already housed Colorado's territorial prison. So the decision was made in Boulder's favor, and the cornerstone of what was to become Old Main was laid in September 1875.

Old Main, as well as a few of the older buildings such as Macky Auditorium, differ from that red-roofed flagstone Tuscan Vernacular Revival architecture for which the university is famous. The initial style of the university was rather more Gothic, much like many well-established colleges on the East Coast. Architect Charles Klauder decided to wrap the buildings in sandstone and tile the roofs of all buildings built after 1921, creating the distinctive architectural motif that CU has clung to, in most areas, ever since. The sandstone gives the institution a sort of "rugged" look that most felt was appropriate for a "western" university. The University of Colorado has since grown from that single building, Old Main, with an initial class of fifteen students, to a campus of forty-six thousand scholars (including seven thousand graduate students and ten thousand faculty members) spread across a sizeable chunk of Boulder's twenty-six square miles.

MACKY AUDITORIUM

It wouldn't be fair to write this chapter without inclusion of the purported hauntings of Macky Auditorium. Let it be said early on, however, that a wide variety of paranormal investigators, sensitives and psychics have roamed the halls on a number of occasions, under different circumstances every time, and none of them reported finding any conclusive evidence of paranormal activity. Nevertheless, the auditorium has gone down in history as being the most haunted building on campus, and those rumors should be given their due, if only for their role in the history of the university.

Born in 1834, Andrew J. Macky found himself in Colorado in 1856, following the rush of settlers pursuing the Pike's Peak Gold Rush. A New York man at heart, Macky had purchased several claims in and around Golden, Colorado. After these initially came up dry, he arrived in 1859 in Boulder, where he took up a plethora of positions, including carpenter, postmaster, treasurer, justice of the peace, school secretary, and clerk of the district court. He finally found his calling when he founded the First National Bank of Boulder in 1877, which he presided over until his death in 1907. As one of Boulder's original settlers, he was well known for being the first to build a frame building in Boulder. His own home at Fourteenth and Pearl doubled as the county courthouse until he built Union

Hall. He also was the first denizen of a brick home, at Twelfth and Pearl, and he helped establish both the city's gas plant and the Boulder Mill and Elevator Company. Macky was a prominent and influential citizen, and everyone who knew him spoke of his dedication to the public interest, as well as his business sense and interest in service opportunities.

Not a college graduate himself, Macky was inspired by the school spirit shown by CU football fans. In 1905, he traveled to Lincoln, Nebraska, to watch an away game between the Buffaloes and the Cornhuskers and was so moved by the fans' devotion to their team—despite an 18–0 loss to the Huskers—that he decided to invest even more than he had already in the future of the university. When he died in 1907, he left $300,000 to the university, the largest gift a Colorado institution had ever seen. A newspaper account of his donation read, "Lacking the advantages of a university education, he was a sincere advocate of higher learning and advanced culture and was often heard to regret that he had not been able to go to college. His generous gift to the university was, in itself, evidence that he was among those rare persons who are willing to give their all that others might enjoy privileges that they had been denied." Thus, the plans for Macky Auditorium were laid at the request of CU president Baker, who wanted something in the style of the "Palazzo Vecchio in Florence, Italy; the King's Chapel in Cambridge, England; the Magdalene Tower in Oxford, England; a Princeton campus building and a New York City church." The ground was broken in 1909, with the cornerstone laid in 1910.

Despite Macky's best intentions, however, the construction didn't exactly go off without a hitch. His adopted daughter, May, had been struck from his will after she married John Rooney against his wishes. She was given $50 and removed from his estate. May sued the university for the portion of his estate that had been donated, and so began a several-year legal battle that the university eventually won. Construction was finally concluded in 1922, with furnishings that included upright wooden seats and a $68,000 organ—the equivalent of almost $800,000 in today's dollars. The two-thousand-seat auditorium has housed Shakespeare Festival rehearsals, graduation ceremonies and Christmas pageants, as well as talks by such luminaries as the Dalai Lama, Archbishop Desmond Tutu and Jane Goodall. As an intimate music venue, audiences have enjoyed concerts by Harry Belafonte, Neil Young, Yo-Yo Ma and R.E.M., as well as countless other events over the years. One of the more harrowing events there, however, took place in the summer of 1966.

Macky Auditorium has long been the subject of haunting rumors, and for good reason.
Photo by Ann Alexander Leggett.

Elaura J. Jacquette, a twenty-one-year-old zoology major, was babysitting. She had just dropped her two charges off at a movie on the Hill, and in an effort to get some serious studying done, she retired to the grass of the west quadrangle, where she spread out her lunch, books and personal belongings. As she settled in for the duration of the movie, CU custodian Joseph Morse approached her. One theory states that he asked for help with an injured bird, but whatever the case, he lured her into Macky Auditorium, up to a tower room, where he beat, raped and murdered her before setting the room on fire. The arson was unsuccessful in covering up the crime, and Morse's own daughters tipped off the police when they later saw him with bloodied clothing. He was convicted and sentenced to 888 years. Morse has since died in prison, offering neither remorse nor explanation for the last day of Jacquette's life and leaving a stain on the history of such a beautiful and historical building on CU campus. There is a plaque memorializing Jacquette located on the lawn where the police found her belongings—it simply reads "Elaura J. Jacquette, 1945–1966," followed by a Roethke quote: "It is neither spring nor summer, it is always."

Of course, when such a brutal event occurs, the details go along the grapevine and become more distorted and expanded as time goes on. The tale is more often recounted as a beautiful young opera singer murdered mid-rehearsal, either singing an aria or playing the organ, and the storytellers are sure to include the blood that covered the walls before the murder struck his match. Regardless, students have reported, sworn even, that they heard the organ playing at all hours, midday or midnight, punctuated by screams. Some have reported seeing a young girl in a white dress float across the stage or down the stairs, and a select few claim that they have seen bloodstains appear on walls or organ keys suddenly, before fading away as though they had never been. A number of professional (and amateur) ghost hunters, psychics and researchers have combed the building, however, and no energy has ever attempted make itself known. Go sit in the auditorium when it's empty, though, and listen for the faint sound of an organ from the practice room above—all those accounts can't have been fabricated, can they?

Sewall Hall

Sewall Hall is a residential hall located on the north side of campus, housing 340 students, all of whom are enrolled in the Sewall Residential Academics Program (SRAP), an offshoot of the College of Arts and Sciences that emphasizes the historical events behind modern culture, targeted toward first-year students interested in both history and culture. The irony is thick here, seeing as the history of Sewall has been so obscured by rumor as to make its connections to modern life almost meaningless.

Joseph A. Sewall was born in Scarborough, Maine, in 1830. In 1852, he graduated with an MD from Massachusetts Medical School, but education proved to be a bigger draw, and he became the principal of the high school in Princeton, Illinois. He was hired as the first president of the University of Colorado in 1877. As one of the institution's two founding faculty members, he also taught chemistry and metallurgy and was paid $3,000 annually for his services in all three areas. He presided over the university for a decade, reappearing periodically in later years to speak on a variety of auspicious occasions such as the university's Quarto Centennial in 1902. Sewall died of a stroke in January 1917, and he is buried with his family in Denver. Sewall Hall, named in his honor, opened in 1935.

Sewall Hall was the first dormitory on campus, and it was built exclusively for female students. It is made up of four wings, each named after an influential woman from the history of the university. Lester is named for Pynk Lester, who was married to the dean of the graduate school (1919–42), the man who later became vice-president and acting president of the university (1921–33). Harding is named after University Regent Minnie Harding, while Bigelow honors Dean of Women (1914–20) Antoinette Bigelow. Finally, Olivia McKenna, who founded the University Women's Club for non-Hellenic women's activities, has her name on the wing now known as McKeehan. Sewall later became the university's first coed dorm and remains a popular option for residence to this day, despite the tales surrounding the building's history.

According to popular hearsay, Sewall Hall was once a funeral home, and it is purportedly a stopping point for many souls from the 1918 flu pandemic en route to the afterlife. Students trade stories of cremation furnaces that have been replaced by freezers and rooms that used to house bodies in various stages of the embalming process. Although it is true that Sewall was repurposed, once upon a time, to house troops and air force personnel during World War II, the hall did not even exist during the infamous influenza epidemic that claimed almost eight thousand lives locally between September 1918 and June 1919.

This outbreak of what was called the Spanish flu claimed more American lives than were slain in battle in World War I and World War II put together, and it has been remembered both nationally and internationally as one of the major pandemics of the twentieth century. Katherine Ann Porter, a columnist for the *Rocky Mountain News*, survived the outbreak despite running a fever of 105 degrees for nine days. Her fictional counterpart, Miranda (from Porter's novel *Pale Horse, Pale Rider*), fought the flu until "there remained of her only a minute fiercely burning particle of being that knew itself alone. This fiery motionless particle set itself unaided to resist destruction. Trust me, the hard unwinking angry point of light said. Trust me. I stay."

In Colorado, influenza was first spotted among military recruits who had reported for duty at the University of Colorado. At the height of the pandemic, Sewall Hall's close neighbor, the Clare Small building, allegedly functioned as a hospital and a morgue for the victims of influenza. However, that, too, is incorrect—that building, originally the Women's Gymnasium, was not built until 1926. Meanwhile, the university had an actual hospital on campus beginning in 1889 (or 1898, depending on the source). Either way, visitors and denizens of both buildings have heard and, in some cases, perpetuated these rumors over the years.

COCKERELL HALL

Theodore Dru Alison Cockerell was born in Norwood, England, in 1866. He was one of six total children born to Brighton coal merchant Sydney John Cockerell. Theodore had an early interest in botany and zoology, a passion that was fed by visits to natural history museums. Unfortunately, he was always a sickly child, and he found he had tuberculosis at the young age of twenty.

Tuberculosis was responsible for a terrifying plurality of American deaths by disease around the turn of the twentieth century. Many doctors in more compact, urban areas, such as much of the East Coast, encouraged their patients to move to higher altitudes with cleaner, drier air, to be closer to nature and away from the squalid cities. As a result, the arid high plains and foothills of Colorado proved to be a mecca for tubercular paupers and intellectuals alike. P.T. Barnum, circus purveyor and part-time Denver resident, remarked, "People come here to die and they can't do it." At an elevation of more than 5,200 feet above sea level, the city of Boulder and the university benefited quite a bit from the disease, as great thinkers of the late nineteenth and early twentieth centuries found themselves accompanying loved ones (or traveling themselves) to Boulder in search of clean air. The poet Robert Frost, for example, became a regular on campus as his daughter, Marjorie, fought the disease. Not only did the otherwise devastating illness provide population growth to Boulder and the surrounding areas, it also helped the economy as ailing TB patients survived and stayed.

Cockerell, like so many others suffering from tuberculosis, left for America in the hopes of finding a climate more suitable for curing his ailment, and in 1887, he began a new life in Colorado. He studied botany in the field there for only three years before returning to England to marry Annie Fenn, the girl he fell in love with before he left. He had spent three years smuggling her letters via her brother, Frederick, due to her father's disapproval of her courtship with "a socialist who had tuberculosis and no reputable house or career." In 1890, Mr. Fenn finally gave his grudging approval to Cockerell and his daughter, and they married, moving to Kingston, Jamaica, where Cockerell curated a museum for a year or so.

After a relapse of tuberculosis, however, he and Annie moved to New Mexico, where Cockerell taught entomology and zoology at New Mexico Agricultural College (now New Mexico State University). After Annie died in childbirth in 1893, Cockerell kept moving north, arriving in Las Vegas, New Mexico, in 1900. He taught at New Mexico Normal University (now Highlands University) there for a few years, marrying Wilmatte Porter in 1903. They relocated to Colorado Springs, where he curated a museum at Colorado College.

The pair ultimately settled in Boulder in 1904. They both taught at the preparatory school on campus as Cockerell also gave university lectures on entomology. He became a full-fledged university professor of zoology in 1906. Arguably the most prolific taxonomist of his time, Cockerell catalogued descriptions of some nine thousand species of insects. He published more than three thousand academic articles, two thirds of which were scientific works on bees, evolution, paleontology and various other animal species, with the other third covering philosophical works such as treatises on social reform and education. Cockerell is most famous for his extensive work on bees, cataloguing more than nine hundred species in Colorado alone. He died in San Diego, California, in 1948.

Built in the 1920s, Cockerell Hall is yet another of CU's numerous residence halls. Instead of catering to students interested in Theodore Cockerell's fields of study, however, residence in Cockerell requires participation in the Engineering Living & Learning Community—in other words, 140 freshmen harboring an interest in engineering and applied sciences. It is apparently home to a few other less lively residents as well, according to the campus rumor mill. There have been reports of a woman in a long nightgown that appears in a third-floor bathroom or up by the attic stairs. This Lady in Gray (or White, or Black, depending on who is telling the tale) is a common theme of stories surrounding Cockerell.

COLLEGE INN

Although this last section of the University of Colorado's paranormal history is not nearly as old as its predecessors, the College Inn is one of the only areas with any "proven" (and we use this term loosely) otherworldly activity. Built in 1964, there is not much available history of the building, except that the university acquired it in 1976 and used it as a conference center. The building was renovated in 2002 for use as overflow housing for students who could not be placed in the available residence halls. The university is, at the time this book was submitted to be published, slated to spend about $1.5 million to demolish the building in the latter half of 2013. This aged and well-loved portion of the university has come to the end of its usefulness, as additions to Willard and Smith Halls, as well as the ever-popular Williams Village student housing, have added more than enough space to accommodate the university's needs.

As a remnant of the 1960s, the ceiling of the College Inn was created using fire-retardant asbestos, a dangerous carcinogen responsible for mesothelioma and lung cancer in those who inhale its long, fibrous crystals. The university estimates it would cost almost $4 million to renovate the Inn: $750,000 to make the building safe and asbestos-free, and the additional $3 million to remodel the interior, as well as replace the out-of-date electrical system, elevators and boilers. The building simply isn't worth that much, and CU has opted for its destruction. Abby Daniels, the executive director of Historic Boulder and one of the Inn's residents in the mid-'90s, affirmed that the preservation committee couldn't find any historic significance in the Inn that might stay its demolition. The nocturnal troubles it has experienced, however, may remain once the building has been demolished, if they have any ties to the land beneath.

Although the building director, having served a decade or so within its walls, knows of no reported traumatic events within the Inn, a number of visitors, employees and media presences in the area have concluded that the building is haunted. The activity seems to center on the south side of the building, primarily on the third floor. People have reported anything from smoke without fire to full-body apparitions, disembodied voices, partial apparitions and bloodstains on the walls. Objects have been moved about while the College Inn stood empty. A few visitors have walked by the elevators en route to their rooms, only to have the doors shoot open to reveal no one inside. Just as abruptly, the doors would close, and the elevator would carry on, with no indication of which floor it was traveling to. Far more eerie, however, is the tale of a late summer evening in July 1999.

The College Inn stood empty, in between conferences. Housekeeping had finished tending to the rooms after the first lecture, and the guests for the next weren't due to arrive until the next afternoon at the earliest. The manager had left for the night, leaving a night man in charge but expecting him to do very little over the course of the evening. In the hallways on each floor, there was a series of globe-shaped lamps on the walls, illuminating signs pointing the residents toward the exits and bathrooms—hundreds of them throughout the whole structure. At some point during the night, every single one of those lamps hit the carpet, gently and without breaking. When the fallen globes were discovered in the morning, the employees were understandably shaken. The night watchman was questioned—he'd heard nothing. There were enough lamps that it took two days to reinstall all of them, so no earthly force could have dislodged them all in the span of one night.

While the College Inn hasn't appeared in the news for any grisly murders or suspicious deaths, for some reason it has kept its hold on its visitors. A creeping chill that grows in the night forces them to retell their nights- or days-long stay whenever they get the chance.

Although there is very little evidence to support some of these purported hauntings and, in some cases, very few real paranormal activities tied to the actual history of these buildings, the University of Colorado at Boulder is certainly one of the more interesting portions of Boulder's history. It housed intellectuals from all over the world, countless students, professors, influential citizens and Colorado pioneers. The campus has grown and changed exponentially over the last 137 years, as would be expected of an institution of its size and caliber, but it still retains its original thumbprint. Its ties to Colorado history are unmistakable and indelible, and for some of its residents—the unearthly ones—it hasn't changed enough to make them leave just yet. From the history come the ghosts, and this history is certainly rife with them.

The Miner's House on Mapleton

The spirits in some houses are not as active as those in others, yet at the same time, their presence can be very profound. This is certainly the case with the Darnalls' house on Mapleton. When the front door of this old home opens, a trip through time begins. It's a journey back to the Victorian era, complete with a front parlor, rich wall coverings and heavy, red velvet draperies. Diana Darnall and her husband made only subtle changes to the house when they purchased it in 1995. Their goal was simple: make the home comfortable and livable while maintaining its rich historic character. The end result is a stunning mixture of beauty and Victorian charm.

The history of the house and its residents is colorful indeed. Built in 1874, the house sits on land that was originally part of a larger tract given as "bounty land," which was granted to military personnel in payment for their services to the United States Army. The General Land Office gave the original tract of land, some 160 acres, to Demetrio Arnuncito in 1866. He was a volunteer soldier who was a tracker with the New Mexican Volunteers in the Navajo Indian wars. The land remained one large parcel until 1873, when the City of Boulder created the North Boulder Addition. Several changes in ownership took place over the next few years. Mary S. Scott purchased the property from Asbury Staples on June 12, 1875, and remained the owner until her death in 1900 at age sixty-five. Based on title transfer records and *Boulder County News* clips from 1874, it seems apparent that Mr. Staples built the house that remains on the site today, although at that time, Mapleton Avenue was known as Hill Street.

As well-respected Boulder citizens, Mary Scott and her husband, Holland, operated a grocery and confectionery store on Pearl Street. Holland was also the manager of McAllister Supply and Lumber at the corner of Fifteenth and Pearl Streets in Boulder. A *Daily Camera* obituary reports that Mary died in the Mapleton house on June 21, 1900.

In 1918, Mr. Otis "Pearl" Pherson moved into the home with his wife, Ida, who worked as a sales clerk in Boulder until she retired. Otis was a colorful character who had made a career of mining gold, silver and tungsten. Bud Chesebro, born in Boulder in 1919, worked for Otis Pherson when he managed the Grand Republic gold mine in Boulder County in 1934. Chesebro thought his boss was a fine fellow. "He expected an honest day's work from you, which was common in those days, but he was a good man to work for. He was one of those people who had no enemies." Before buying the Mapleton house, Pherson spent his early years in various booming mining camps, including those in Creede and Cripple Creek.

For more than sixty years the Phersons lived in the Mapleton house, and Otis, growing older, began to write of his long, interesting life. Locals report that he had a fascination with electricity, and he would expound on his theories to whoever would listen. An amateur historian, he was also very interested in ghosts and told stories about Boulder's haunted locations. Well known for the many colorful and pointed letters he wrote to the editor of the *Daily Camera*, a sometimes cantankerous Mr. Pherson delighted in sitting on the front porch of his home talking to passersby. He died in the house at age ninety-five. (Ida, who preceded her husband in death, died at Boulder Community Hospital at age ninety-two.) Many years later, when Diana Darnall and her husband took possession of the house, they found old mining tools and equipment in the cellar, a testament to Mr. Pherson's long mining career.

While psychic Krista Socash was interpreting the resident spirit in the home for the 1999 Historic Boulder Spirit Tour, some very interesting and bone-chilling events occurred that validated the home's history. It was a delightful, crisp October evening as people began arriving at the house on Mapleton for the tour. As the first tour group entered the home, the people assembled in the front room, sitting in what was once the formal parlor. According to Krista, a spirit immediately presented itself to her as a miner. Despite not knowing anything about the home before her visit, Krista sensed a hardworking man, very basic in his principles, who led a simple and honest life. Even though it had never made itself known to Diana or her husband, the spirit gave Krista very strong echoes of the past.

The spirit of miner Otis "Pearl" Pherson may inhabit his house on Mapleton Avenue. *Photo by Ann Alexander Leggett.*

During the tour, Krista stood by the front window as she described the essence of the man's spirit that inhabited the home. The window, which faces south, is framed by heavy velvet drapes. Directly to the left of the window hangs a handsome pencil portrait of Mr. Pherson as a child. Diana found the portrait of Otis in the basement of the home and later had it framed.

Krista's talk to the tour group was very basic and included the phrase, "He led a very simple life," for in fact this was the vibration she had sensed very strongly. The phrase, however, did not seem to please the spirit. As soon as she uttered those words, the front porch light flickered and went out, leaving the next group waiting on the porch in the dark. Thinking that the light bulb had burned out, Krista continued her talk as volunteers and those waiting in line scrambled to replace the bulb.

When that group entered the front room, it was treated to Krista's same interpretation of the spirit inhabiting the house. Her talk didn't vary much, and when she got to the part about the man living a very simple life, the front porch light flickered and went out once again. The group had no idea what was happening, but Krista silently made the connection.

By the time the next group of visitors had entered and assembled in the front room, Krista knew that the spirit was disgruntled. This time, when she got to the "simple life" line, the brass tieback holding the curtains fell out of the wall and came crashing to the floor. The tour group jumped in fright, and some, thinking it was just a bit too scary, left the room. Others stayed and watched in fascination as Krista turned and spoke to the spirit directly, apologizing for misinterpreting his feelings. "I realized that the spirit was not happy with the way I had been describing him, so I turned to where the tieback had fallen and spoke to him. I apologized for describing his life as simple, and all activity stopped. He made his point known." The tieback that fell was located directly under the portrait of Otis Pherson, a man who may not have led as uncomplicated a life as it seemed.

The activity in the front room stopped, but there was another presence in the house making itself known. A volunteer helping with tour groups was surprised by the strong scent of roses emanating from the back rooms of the home. Not a single rose was in sight, yet Krista smelled the overpowering fragrance as well. "A female presence, not as prominent as the spirit in the front parlor, was near the library/TV room. She came and went throughout the night," Krista said. Was it perhaps the spirit of Mary Scott?

Despite the crashing curtain tieback, Diana always felt very positive vibrations about the house. It gave her a feeling of happiness and calm. But she also respected the fact that her house will always have a very strong connection with the past, with a life of its own, and with spirits that still call the house on Mapleton their home.

"Boom Days, on the Banks of Cripple Creek," by O.P. Pherson

Back in the early ninetys
In a craze strong for Gold,
Thrilling dreams of fortune,
Searching for wealth untold,
Came a herd of hardy strangers
In a stream o'er the land
Each in a mighty hurry
So they'd be on hand.
Fired with tales of riches
The miner with his pick,
From camps up in the Rockies
Rushed for Cripple Creek.

THE OLD BOULDER HOMESTEAD

Susan was in the second grade when she moved into the north Boulder farmhouse with her parents and two brothers. The classic little red brick farmhouse was right out of a storybook. Surrounded by lovely gardens—including blackberry brambles, thick lilacs and cherry trees—the old house was the center of what used to be a working farm. The five-acre parcel still had a well house with shelves for cooling canned goods, a milk storage house, coal and tool sheds, a chicken house, a spider-ridden outhouse and a huge barn. The original homestead house still stood on the grounds. "A tiny, one-room affair," as Susan described it.

Mr. Skinner, a Boulder bricklayer, built the farmhouse at the turn of the century and sold it in 1938 to a man who went by the name Tungsten. Along with his sons, Tungsten worked in the mines all day and returned to the farm in the evenings to milk their thirty cows. He lived on the property with his wife, Alice Mae, until his death, and she continued to live in the house until Susan's parents bought it in 1962.

The outbuildings on the property were great for exploring, and Susan and her brothers loved the old place. Susan's mother particularly adored the bright and cozy little kitchen with the wood stove. Susan never forgot the thermometer on the old stove with a picture of a chick emerging from a broken shell. A pump over the timeworn sink brought water from the well, and an attached lean-to housed a small claw-footed tub. In addition to the kitchen, the house had two small bedrooms tucked into the upstairs dormers, a dining area and a small sitting area downstairs. It was a step back in time.

Since the kitchen was the center of activity in the house, it was there that the family first realized that they were not alone. Two walls of the kitchen were spanned with windows of multipaned glass, a feature Susan's mother loved. When her mother observed that on some days she could see her reflection in only one of the windows, however, the family began to wonder what was going on. While preparing meals, her mother also heard sounds of walking and shuffling throughout the house. Although Susan never had reason to doubt her mother's experiences, she couldn't help but note that, strangely, her mother was always alone when these things happened.

With three active children, the house soon proved to be too small. In 1965, Susan's father tore down the old house and built a new ranch-style house on the site. The western two-thirds of the new house was constructed on

This old family homestead in north Boulder was home to some of the city's scariest hauntings. *Private collection.*

the same spot as the original little red farmhouse. "Things really started to happen when we tore down the old house," Susan recalled. "We'd be sitting on the patio, which is where the original kitchen stood, and all of a sudden the dogs would jump up, tails wagging, and rush to the same spot and look up. It was as though they were greeting nonexistent guests. This became so commonplace that we didn't make much of it after a while."

Then there was what Susan referred to as "the whistler." "For a long time, the sound of someone whistling in a sing-songy voice followed me through the house. Sometimes it was outside a window, sometimes it followed me down the hall. It was just another one of those strange things that we lived with."

As the children grew older, things got creepier. On one particularly cold New Year's Eve when Susan was babysitting her younger brother, she heard a racket in the front of the house. There were terrible, unimaginable sounds that she would still have difficulty describing even years later. Running into the living room, Susan saw the family's small terrier being physically lifted into the air and repeatedly thrown into a chair by something invisible. "It was terrifying. I couldn't believe what I was seeing. I ran to the phone and called my parents, who were just up the street. When my father arrived, he had to physically wrestle the dog from an unseen force." The dog, though obviously shaken, was unharmed. The rest of the family was shaken as well and could not come up with any explanation for what had happened.

For reasons unknown, the hauntings seem to be most prevalent during the Christmas holidays, particularly on New Year's Eve. "On several New Year's, when we'd have family visiting, we'd always have strange experiences. And the funny thing was that everyone always heard or saw something different. One of us would hear a loud banging on a railing, another would hear footsteps or see doors opening and closing on their own," Susan remembered.

Susan moved away from home when she was nineteen, not long after her brothers. She soon married and began a family of her own, and during that time, she and her husband returned and bought the homestead property and its house from her mother. For a time, the extended family shared their home. The ghostly experiences continued, and it was during those days, when Susan's children were young, that some of the encounters became very frightening.

"One day, when my daughter was almost two years old, I was cleaning up and she was playing with a little purse, putting her toys and things in it. She asked me to hold it, and I said that I was too busy. So she said to me, 'Then I'll give it to the man.' She turned and walked across the room, stopped, looked up and said to something invisible to me, 'Can you hold this? Oh, I'm sorry.' I was stunned. 'What did the man say?' I asked. 'He said he can't hold things anymore,' she answered."

From the beginning, Susan's children seemed to be sensitive to the spirits in the house. When her son was about five years old, he was playing in one of the bedrooms in the home when he suddenly came running from the room in search of his grandmother. "There are holes in the carpet, and little men are coming out!" he cried breathlessly. Things were about to get even stranger.

One day, Susan's young daughter heard a baby. Not a baby on the television or walking by outside with its mother, but a baby on the speakerphone. "She came to me one day and said she had been listening to a baby crying on the phone," Susan recalled. "Sure enough, the phone was not off the hook, but the sound of a wailing, moaning child was coming from the speaker. I kept unplugging the phone, thinking that it was picking up a radio signal, but it lasted for almost an hour."

Lots of strange activity revolved around one room in the house where both of Susan's brothers had slept at one time or another. Her older brother had finally refused to sleep in the room anymore because he kept having unnerving out-of-body floating experiences. The room became a studio for Susan's artist husband and was declared off-limits for sleeping. While working, her husband would hear tremendous fighting and screaming coming from the rest of the house. "He'd burst out into the hall and say, 'What in the world is all the commotion?' And we'd all be sitting in the living room reading," Susan said.

"I had a brother who had some troubled years when he was a teenager," Susan explained. "One day, he and my mother got into a huge fight, and he left the house very upset. My mother called my other brother, who lived nearby, and asked him to come over because she had been so upset by the row. My young daughter was at home that day as well." Her brother stopped what he was doing and started on his way, having no idea of what he would find when he arrived.

According to Susan, her mother and daughter sat down on the top of the steps, waiting for his arrival, when they started to hear the strangest sounds. "My mother heard a machine-like sound. And my daughter heard what she described as a squealing pig. Immediately, the walls of the stairway where they were sitting started to move back and forth and bend as though they were actually breathing. They heaved and pitched until nails popped from the walls. They sat frozen in fear, and it continued until my brother arrived almost five minutes later. As soon as he opened the front door, it stopped. He found them, still sitting on the stairs, surrounded by the nails that littered the floor."

Susan's children are older now, but they still remember their ghostly encounters in the house, which have become fewer and fewer as the years go by. "Doors still slam," Susan said, "and when I'm in the kitchen alone, something tugs at my shirt from time to time." By all accounts, however, the more violent activity has subsided.

Why didn't they ever leave the house? According to Susan, it was just never feasible. "At first, the hauntings happened so infrequently. Then my parents divorced, the house needed lots of work and it just wasn't an option to move. We still love the place, and we feel that the unhappy incidents have abated because of our strength as a loving family. Besides, the little farm was always our dream come true."

THE BLACK DERBY HAT

Anyone who has ever driven Highway 93 from Boulder to Golden knows what a desolate piece of road it can be. Ever-changing weather conditions along the twisting, turning road can bring howling winds, blinding blizzards or dense fog at a moment's notice. Even in deceptively fair weather, the remote route combined with the loneliness of the drive can play tricks on one's weary mind. The constant need to stay alert for the hazards in the path can stretch the nerves to a breaking point. It should come as no surprise, then, that many weary travelers might be tempted to pick up a hitchhiker along that stretch just for the company, even in the dark of night, only to see some things that just can't be explained.

There wasn't much of a moon on that July night in 1881 as a Colorado Central train ran on the tracks just outside Boulder. With a full load of passengers and freight on board, the train chugged along monotonously. The engineer, from his high perch in the locomotive, was enjoying the warm summer evening talking with the train's fireman when something on the track ahead suddenly caught his eye. A human figure appeared in the distance. "My God, there's a man on the track!" he shouted. The engineer pulled the brakes, and the train came to a screeching halt, awakening the passengers from their slumber. Crew members bolted from the train to discover what they had feared. Blood and bits of tissue on the cowcatcher confirmed that they had hit someone or something, but there was no body. Fanning out with lanterns in hand, the crew searched the tall grass along the tracks and the fields next to the train to no avail. Finally, one searcher called out a discovery. It was not the body of a man, however, but a freshly killed deer carcass. Could that have been what the engineer saw, or had the deer been killed by an earlier train? The crew was debating the mystery and whether to continue the search when the conductor walked into the circle of men holding a black derby hat with a red feather in the silk band. Here begins the story of the ghost on Highway 93.

The Colorado Central Railroad was originally established to carry gold down from the mountains during the heady days of the Pikes Peak Gold Rush (later called simply the Colorado Gold Rush). Connecting the young cities of the Plains to the mining towns of Idaho Springs, Central City and Black Hawk, it carried a steady stream of supplies and prospectors eager to find their fortunes. The railroad ran near the present route of the highway connecting Golden to Boulder. Hugging the

It quickly became known that the train was being haunted by a ghost wearing a black derby hat with a gray band and red feather, image circa 1883. *Carnegie Branch Library for Local History, Boulder Historical Society Collection.*

foothills to the west before angling northeast through Boulder, Louisville and Lafayette en route to Cheyenne, Wyoming, the train was a popular route with travelers. Colorado Central president Mr. W.A.H. Loveland, for whom the city of Loveland and Loveland Pass are named, promoted this line as the preferred route to access the city of Golden, which he saw as the new center of commerce in the state.

The morning following the discovery of the black derby hat, Jefferson County coroner Dr. Joseph Anderson, along with a party of men, searched the area adjacent to the tracks. More remnants of the unlucky deer were found, but still no human body. As the temperature rose that afternoon, the search was finally called off. Just then, one of the men made a grisly discovery. A piece of linen collar with a red ruby button lay wedged between the tracks. Now clearly perplexed, the authorities still had no body. Several

Those familiar with the tale still watch for a ghostly figure walking along Highway 93 at night. *Photo by Ann Alexander Leggett.*

months later, with no further clues to work with, the case was closed. It was actually just the beginning.

About a month later, train passengers aboard the Colorado Central route to and from Golden began to report seeing an apparition. All accounts agreed that the vision of the man and his accompanying odor of death were certainly foul. Women would faint at the sight of a man appearing in the seats across from them. Unexplained events and strange sounds aboard the train were attributed to the malevolent spirit, who grew more violent and aggressive in his hauntings of the train cars. Window shades moved up and down repeatedly, dishes in the club car crashed to the floor for no apparent reason and glass lamps burst. Mysterious fires broke out in several of the cars, and passengers heard wailing and moaning from the roof of the train. The ghost seemed to enjoy playing havoc with the passengers, and it quickly became common knowledge that a spirit—a man wearing a black derby hat with a gray band and red feather—was haunting the train.

The apparition of the man in a derby hat was appearing regularly not just on the train but also along the tracks near the scene of the accident. Travelers on the road that ran near the line also reported seeing the apparition walking along the tracks at dusk, only to see him fade away.

The spirit continued to haunt the train and passersby along the route for several years, until with time the sightings became few and far between. In 1890, the rail line was abandoned, and traffic on the gravel wagon road, eventually to become Highway 93, steadily increased. Soon, travelers in wagons and later in cars began to report a man with a derby hat hitchhiking at night along the dark road near the creek. Sometimes the apparition carried a lantern and waved it as if motioning for help. According to the drivers who stopped to help him, the phantom hitchhiker would explain that a train had derailed and that he needed to get into town to report the accident. Once the man got into an automobile, however, drivers would look over at their passenger only to see his image dissolve before their eyes. Over the years, the sightings have also included reports of a headless man hitchhiking along the same stretch of road, in some cases holding not a lantern but his own head by the hair. A gruesome sight indeed.

The legend of the haunting persists to this day, with occasional sightings of the man in the derby hat. You might see a white vaporous shape or, as you pass by the spot where he may have met his demise just outside Boulder, get the feeling of the hair standing up on the back of your neck.

The Grill Mansion

A s you finish your drink at the Corner Bar inside the Hotel Boulderado, you might be thinking about the next point of interest on your visit to downtown Boulder. The Pearl Street Mall draws quite a crowd, as do the Hill and the University of Colorado campus, but you aren't necessarily looking to remain on the beaten path—the really interesting locations are those that few know about. Head north on Thirteenth, take a left on Mapleton and walk west a block or two until you hit Broadway: there, some sixty feet back from the sidewalk and surrounded by trees, resides the infamous Grill Mansion. The house lords over the entrance to the Mapleton neighborhood, once *the* place to live in Boulder. The serious and imposing tone of the mansion's brick façade is somewhat lessened by the beautiful and meandering walkway from the corner of Broadway and Mapleton up to its overlarge front porch. To say that it "squats" or "lurks" would be to misconstrue the beauty of its symmetrical Palladian-influenced architecture, but its presence has a certain foreboding weight to it, as though the building is truly the intimidating gatekeeper to one of Boulder's more interesting historical neighborhoods.

We knew from the beginning that we were going to have to devote a chapter of this book to this formidable house. It has always been called the Grill Mansion, despite the fact that Ernest Grill owned the house for only some twenty years out of the last century. Since its construction, it has seen use as a residence, as law offices and, for the better part of its life, as a series of increasingly successful mortuaries. As we commenced our research, we were to hear over and over, "Oh, yes, the Grill is definitely haunted." But by whom or by what? Dark hints and vague allusions were all that greeted our inquiries. More than once, the people we interviewed simply declined to discuss any details. Much like Trezise's old undertaking company, the Grill Mansion can only be described as the stuff of uneasy dreams and neighborhood legends.

Finished in 1907 by the entrepreneur Ernest Grill, the mansion was constructed on the site of previous homes, Reverend Nathan Thompson's house earliest among them. As the first settled pastor of any Boulder church, Reverend Thompson ministered in particular to the First Congregational Church, established in 1865. He built this house for his family, and they resided there until they left the town in 1875. The house and lot were then purchased by Dr. Charles C. Brace.

Dr. Brace was a well-established member of the Boulder community, having married two-time mayor J.P. Maxwell's sister, Mabel. The Maxwells were one of the more prominent pioneer families at the time—J.P. built a toll road up Boulder Canyon, was appointed the first state engineer of Colorado and surveyed Boulder's first municipal water supply. His stepmother, Martha, revolutionized taxidermy, as well as museum display methods, even opening a museum of natural history in Boulder in 1868. Dr. Brace may have originally benefited from his ties to such a family, but he soon came into his own, becoming involved in the production of "Denver Mud," or antiphlogistine, a clay poultice used to treat boils and sore throats. Denver Mud became a multimillion-dollar enterprise, and Brace and his family ended up in New York.

Long before Denver Mud took off, and before the Maxwells had even ridden into Boulder, Ernest Grill was born in Linneus, Missouri, on December 1, 1859. His father moved that same year to Colorado and, in 1862, brought his family out to join him in his establishment of a wholesale grocery. The Grill family settled near the site of what was to become Limon and lived there for a year before traveling the one hundred miles northwest to Denver. They finally arrived in Boulder in 1875. A young Ernest found himself attending prep school in Denver and enrolled in one of the University of Colorado's inaugural classes. After two years at CU Boulder, Grill moved to Ercurt, Germany, to continue his education. He returned to Colorado in the mid-1880s and began farming in Berthoud around the time of that town's establishment. He soon moved into the mountains and spent the next fifteen memorable years in the booming mining town of Silverton, working for Otto Mears.

Silverton saw Grill's arrival in 1886 with only ten dollars in his pocket; he resolved to get by on one meal per day until he found a job. That job came

The Grill Mansion, with its rich history, has long been the subject of haunting rumors in Boulder, perhaps mainly because it is such a grand and imposing building. *Photo by Ann Alexander Leggett.*

from Mears Transportation Company, and Grill was hired to herd horses at night. His memoirs recorded some of the harsh conditions during the early part of his stay: "There had been a big snow slide in the canyon ten miles from Silverton, covering the track to a depth of 60 feet. They had to shovel the snow out in benches, each man pitching the snow to a man above him a height of eight feet." He managed his herds for about a week before he realized that they were starving, and he stomped into the office with the intention of quitting. He announced, "Bad as [he] needed a job, [he] did not propose to starve a lot of dumb animals to hold it." Otto Mears overheard, asked for an explanation and found out that his superintendent had been withholding horse feed to cut costs. As simple as that, Ernest Grill made a lifelong enemy in the superintendent and a lifelong friend in Otto Mears.

Over the course of the next fifteen years, Grill spent more than 50 percent of his working hours in the saddle of his horse, Dick, a present from Mears. He freighted goods into and out of Silverton until Mears had established enough railroad track to give up the wagon freight trade. Right around this time, Grill found a schoolteacher in Red Mountain with whom he decided he wanted to spend the rest of his life. He was married to Lurene "Lulu" Whistler on Halloween in 1888, and they had three children: Ernest Jr., Helen and Margaret.

Grill stayed on with Mears as a road-master for a few more years, making money by purchasing grain and hay on the side for clients and shipping it with his scheduled trainloads for Mears. Eventually, he established his own lumber and feed business in Silverton, and he bought out the LaPlata Coke and Coal Company to supplement his own trade. Grill claimed that he "moved to Boulder to put [his] children in school there, but they ended up going to Stanford, Vassar and Lawrenceville." His return to Boulder around the turn of the century heralded the establishment of the Grill Lumber Company, later called the Builder's Supply Company. A few years later, Grill decided that he needed an abode that suited his stature and interests and set out to find the perfect parcel of land on which to build "a pretty good home"—the Grill Mansion.

Ernest Grill purchased the land at the corner of Mapleton and Broadway from Dr. Brace in 1904, razed the existing structure and began the three-year construction process that would yield the beautiful and formidable Grill Mansion. It's quite possible that Lulu had a hand in the design—some later tales of the mansion mention the spirit of a woman distressed at subsequent renovations. The application for landmark status cites the architect as Arthur E. Saunders and lists the house as a representation of the work of a master—

the style is Italian Renaissance Revival, and the layout certainly speaks to a Palladian conception with a few tasteful variations. The most striking feature is the massive stone porch, with a broad archway supported by stone pillars that is echoed by another archway above the second-floor windows and a third wooden arch directly above the front dormer. The building is largely constructed of tan brick, although overall, a visual impression of darkened spaces is created by the deeply shaded portions and an emphasis on the dark wood. The roof is an Italianate green tile. The interior is largely characterized by dark stained woodwork juxtaposed with a rare soft yellow pine floor, white tile fireplaces and numerous clear and stained-glass windows. The structure includes thirty rooms and is aptly labeled a mansion.

For all its grandeur and majesty, Ernest Grill and his family lived in the mansion only until 1923, when he sold it to R.J. Bruner and William Tippett. Grill was a member of the Masons, the Elks and Sons of the American Revolution during his time in Boulder, but not much information about him is available after the sale of his house—he almost seems to have disappeared after he signed the bill of sale, with the exception of the notice of his death. He died in Palm Springs on March 22, 1957, at the then incredible age of ninety-eight.

Over the many decades of its use as a place of business, the Grill Mansion would see a dizzying succession of owners and partners, many of them in the funeral profession. Immediately upon their receipt of the deed, R.J. Bruner and William Tippett took the Grill Mansion and transformed it into Tippett-Bruner Mortuary. Bruner stayed in the mansion for only three years before selling his share of the business to George R.A. Hall, reportedly the only mortician in Colorado ever to have buried a man three times.

George Rass Asbury Hall was born on September 1, 1878, in Gower, Missouri. His family moved to Cripple Creek, Colorado, in 1892. Only five short years later, at the age of nineteen, Hall completed the requisite education and became a licensed embalmer and mortician. Hall, along with John Trezise and William Tippett, collaborated in the founding of the Colorado Funeral Directors Association in 1898. For almost three decades, Hall provided funeral services in Trinidad and Cripple Creek, as well as Victor, Colorado, where he became well known for officiating three burials for the same man.

In 1906, it seems that a miner named John McEachern took out three $1,000 life insurance policies in his own name right around the time that an accident in the Portland Mine claimed the life of his acquaintance and fellow miner, Bob Speed. Mr. Speed was buried by George Hall in the

Protestant section of the cemetery in Victor. McEachern and a friend secretly disinterred Speed, moved his body to Three Jacks Tunnel and surrounded it with chunks of hair that they had shorn from a red steer, to approximate the color of McEachern's flame-red hair. The two men rigged an explosion and collapsed a good portion of the tunnel. Speed's long-dead body was identified as McEachern's and was buried—again by George Hall—in the Catholic section of Victor's cemetery.

The postman, who'd served as a pallbearer at both funerals, was in the process of delivering the three $1,000 insurance checks to McEachern's house when he saw the supposed decedent sitting in his own kitchen, alive and well. The postman reported McEachern to the sheriff, and McEachern was arrested. Bob Speed's widow, wildly anti-Catholic like her late husband, demanded that he be removed from the Catholic section, and so Hall officiated a third funeral for Speed's corpse, reinterring him in the Protestant section. Possible malfeasance notwithstanding, Hall boasted of that story for the rest of his life.

Not long before the infamous triple funeral, George Hall married Isabelle McCollough Wood of Glasgow, Scotland, in Denver on November 30, 1905. The couple had three daughters, Evelyn, Roberta and Eleanor. In 1926, Hall moved to Boulder to take advantage of its burgeoning school district, and he formed a partnership with William Tippett by purchasing Milo Rice's share in the mortuary. Exactly when R.J. Bruner sold out and Rice came into the business is unclear, as many of the burial records show funerals as officiated by various and contradictory combinations of the names of the morticians and their evolving partnerships—let it suffice to say that Tippett was the primary business owner and Rice and Bruner his partners from 1923 to 1926.

It is easy to imagine how frustrating the bookkeeping must have been, and indeed there are stories of a harried accountant inhabiting the attic of the mansion, juggling the dusty books even in the afterlife. As of 1926, the Grill Mansion became home to the Tippett-Hall Mortuary, although it remained that way for only four years until William Tippett's death in 1930. Leslie B. Kelso purchased Tippett's share, and once more the mansion was renamed—it became the Hall-Kelso Mortuary.

Leslie Kelso was born on July 25, 1885, in Courtland, Nebraska. His parents, Lewis and Rebecca, moved Leslie and his three brothers to Boulder in 1902. Shortly after his arrival in Boulder, Kelso graduated from Old Prep School (now Boulder High) and began working toward a career as an undertaker. He became apprenticed to John Trezise between 1908 and 1910, succeeding Trezise as Boulder County coroner in 1912. Over the next ten years, Kelso sparred with another well-established Boulder mortician, A.E. Howe, for the coroner's seat. He left Trezise Undertaking after Trezise died during the 1918 influenza pandemic. No longer just an apprentice, Kelso opened his own undertaking business at 1545 Pearl and stayed there until 1930, when he purchased Tippett's half of the Tippett-Hall Mortuary and became one-half of the newly minted Hall-Kelso Mortuary. He remained at that location until his retirement in 1945 and spent his remaining summers in Boulder and his winters in Florida. On July 1, 1968, Kelso passed away in Boulder and was buried at Green Mountain Cemetery.

Just one year prior to Kelso's retirement, Hall retired from the funeral business himself and sold his half of Hall-Kelso to Howard McClure of Kansas. McClure arrived in Boulder from Oberlin, Kansas, where he had been both county coroner and a funeral director for quite some time. Only one month after his entrée into the Hall-Kelso Mortuary (which he had immediately renamed McClure Funeral Home), he sold his portion to John F. Allardice. Born in Pennsylvania on June 15, 1907, Allardice had moved to Denver by the age of fifteen. He attended South Denver High and Denver University before striking out to join the oddly attractive undertaking industry. He was exceptionally successful in the profession, working in a variety of Colorado regions before arriving in Boulder in the early 1940s. He joined the Lions, Elks, Masons, Knights Templar and the Order of the Eastern Star, and he also served as president of the chamber of commerce for two years. In 1944, he purchased McClure's share of the McClure Funeral Home (still popularly known as the Hall-Kelso Mortuary, for the most part, despite McClure's efforts to relabel it), and he bought Kelso out just a year later, renaming the business the Allardice Mortuary. In 1946, he took Ross Hibbard as his partner and so formed the Allardice-Hibbard Mortuary.

Ross Hibbard, of Gerard, Kansas, had a long and lucrative career in Kansas both on his own and working for a furniture and undertaking firm (a logical and very popular pairing in the early twentieth century). He came to Boulder for health reasons in 1922 and became Allardice's partner. Allardice sold his own share to J. Walter Geddes in 1954, and the mansion was renamed yet again: the Geddes-Hibbard Mortuary. Hibbard stayed on until 1964 and died in 1968. Geddes joined him in death in 1968, and Robert A. Crist took over the mortuary for its final iteration of a funeral home, Crist Mortuary. Crist had served in World War II and graduated from the School of Mortuary Science in Kansas City, Kansas, after he returned from duty as a pilot overseas. His career was varied, serving not only as assistant coroner in four different Colorado counties (El Paso, Otero, Adams and Larimer) but also as deputy sheriff of Otero County for nine years.

Crist Mortuary is still in business, although it has since relocated out onto the Longmont Diagonal. In 1972, the 2305 Partnership was formed by Jim Leach, Gene Arnold and Bruce Downing; they purchased the Grill Mansion and converted it into office space. The mansion has been home to a series of offices ever since and is now almost entirely dedicated to a group of law offices.

Whispers of hauntings in this house abound, but it was almost impossible to find anyone willing to share their experiences. A few phone calls to the law offices yielded a consistent series of short responses: "I've never seen anything, and I don't know anyone who would talk to you if they had." Lawyers are both busy and very careful of their reputations, so getting any current stories would prove to be more difficult than had been originally anticipated. A few more carefully probing inquiries finally yielded something that could be of use: the psychics who visited the house with Historic Boulder's Ghost Walk, Ghost Talk tour mentioned that the accountant from the mortuary was residing in the attic and that the woman who built the house is mad that it isn't her house anymore.

As you've read here, the history of the Grill Mansion becomes convoluted from the day it was turned into a mortuary—it would be impossible to track down the accountant of any particular partnership with any certainty, as it changed hands so many times over such a long period of time. There can be little doubt, however, that the spirit of any accountant tasked with keeping track of so many transitions might linger on the premises, for better or worse.

That leaves Lurene "Lulu" Grill as being the easiest individual to identify, and she is upset that the house is no longer hers. That particular attitude makes the house's early history even more interesting. Why did Grill build such an extravagant residence and then sell it, disappearing into relative obscurity? How odd that Tippett and Bruner chose that family residence to be a mortuary instead of acquiring a building more specifically designed for undertaking. Most curiously, why would Lulu choose to spend her afterlife, disgruntled, in the house she inhabited for only sixteen years? She appeared both distressed and angry to the psychics who volunteered, so we find ourselves questioning what, exactly, happened in this house to tie her to it for so many years after her death.

Many people have the misconception that mortuaries are among the most haunted of places in this day and age. Interestingly, however, the two spirits who are claimed to inhabit the Grill Mansion are those of actual denizens of the house during their lifetimes. Psychics and sensitives agree: ghosts return to where they are emotionally attached. No matter how many corpses passed through the doors of each mortuary housed within the Grill Mansion, only someone who cared about that house a great deal would choose to spend his or her afterlife in it.

SHORT BUT SPOOKY

This chapter focuses on a few haunted locations that are slightly lacking in history and yet have incredible circumstances surrounding them. One exception is the Hannah Barker House. The paranormal happenings at that house are interesting enough to warrant its inclusion in our manuscript, but the history has been so widely circulated that it would be tough to describe any nuance of the history that hasn't yet been told. As a result, we give an abbreviated version here along with some paranormal tidbits.

All of these tales are largely from anonymous homeowners, friends, tenants or regulars of each location, and they were enough to catch our ear. We hope that these short tales will draw you in as they did us and give you goose bumps just as sharply as the previous chapters.

THE MEDITATION ROOM

The hauntings at the house on Lincoln Place at first seemed so benign. Roommates Andy and Kate lived there in the late 1980s, and it didn't take long after they moved in for them to realize that something was amiss. The three-bedroom home still stands in the neighborhood where elegant Tudor homes, small bungalows and modern remodels coexist nicely.

They say that the ghost activity began with air currents. Actually, wind might be a better word to describe the mysterious drafts that blew through

Most of Boulder's spooky stories are steeped in history. The city's historic Columbia Cemetery, located on Ninth Street, is home to the remains of many of Boulder's colorful and famous citizens. *Photo by Ann Alexander Leggett.*

the house when no windows or doors were open. These drafts actually blew papers off tables, and with their sudden arrival, Kate and Andy felt a presence arrive with them, although they could never really explain it in words. Throughout summer and winter, the drafts blew through the home. It was something they learned to live with and even joked about. The hauntings soon began to take another form. The radio would start to play—not a result of anyone touching the actual radio, mind you, but in the wee hours, usually around two or three o'clock in the morning. The radio would come alive, at top volume, jolting Andy and Kate awake. Curiously, the radio stations in these middle-of-the-night hauntings were not the same stations normally listened to by the couple.

Then events took a turn for the worse. One evening, with houseguests in town, Kate offered her room to her visitors and went off to sleep in a small upstairs room. She called the room the "Meditation Room." It was square in shape with a corner built out, probably for a vent or pipe of some sort. Kate still remembers the dream she was having that night when she was so rudely awakened: she was at a party, and she was happy and having a great time. She began to dream that her head was being lifted, and at that point, her dream became reality. As she was sleeping, the ghost raised her body and threw her against the wall. Hitting the room's sharp corner, the blow of her body slamming against the wall awakened the guests in the next room, who ran in to find her bleeding from the forehead.

Kate has never been able to explain the apparent sudden violence shown by the ghost, except that it was obviously upset that she was sleeping in the room. Needless to say, she never slept there again, and shortly afterward, Kate and Andy moved out of the house.

"After I was thrown, I entered that room more cautiously," Kate said. "We were scheduled to move a few weeks after it happened. I was definitely happy to be leaving." To this day, the mystery of the Lincoln Place ghost and the Meditation Room on the upper floor remain just that—a mystery never to be solved.

THE QUERULOUS HOUSEGUEST

Just a stone's throw from the infamous Kohler House sits another residence from another time. Not quite as old, the house was built in the 1920s, and very little was known about its past until it came into the hands of the current owner's friend. The house is modest and conventional, a prime example of Boulder residential life in the early '20s. There is an attic room that peeks out over the front lawn and a small but well-kept porch that makes the whole edifice both quaint and also rather familiarly inviting. A therapist now owns the little house, and the aura of warmth and friendliness extends to within the house as well. The attic room is often rented out to students of the nearby Rolfing school and has seen a number of tenants since the current owner settled in. One guest that has remained fairly constant, however, is the spirit of a teenage girl that seems to have made the attic room her semipermanent home.

Once wallpapered in red and white polka dots, the room has a blurry past. The story is that sometime between 1920 and 1940, a thirteen- or fourteen-year-old girl lived there, spent some time there or possibly even spent her last days there. She has been known to "bother" the tenants, from time to time—not all of them, but a select few. The "bothering" includes, but is not limited to, the spirit watching the tenant fall asleep, watching them until they wake up or (on a rare occasion) causing the bed to rise a few inches into the air and fall back to the floor. She has been seen by a large number of the tenants of the attic, despite their varieties in age, gender, experience, hometown, career path and personality type. The interesting part of this paranormal activity, however, is the common denominator—she only appears to people who either have recently questioned or are currently questioning their sexuality. The owner remarked, "She really only bothers people who are having issues around sexual identity, or sexuality in general...she especially is fond of lesbians."

The house owner has mentioned that while the incidents have lately decreased in frequency, they have stayed consistent to the pattern: someone moves in and isn't told about the possibility of an otherworldly bunkmate. The owner is probably not aware of the tenant's sexual orientation right off the bat. Some time passes, and pretty soon, both topics are broached over the course of a conversation or two about interesting coincidences because the new resident has been visited by the spirit. After all, having one's bed raised up off the floor by some unknown force is certainly something to bring up with the landlord.

The owner of this particular Pine Street house doesn't mind the visitor at all—in fact, she is viewed as merely an interesting side note in an otherwise "normal" and inviting household. The questions have been raised, however, as to who the girl is and where she came from. Why is she attached to this house, and why is she so interested in the sexual preferences of her roommates? It's certainly an interesting twist in paranormal activity that we had not encountered before.

THE WELL-ESTABLISHED BUSINESSWOMAN

It would be unfair to all interested parties if we did not include the story of Hannah Barker in the pages of this publication. We will preface this section, however, with a disclaimer: this blurb, if you will, doesn't nearly do the history justice. At the time this manuscript went to press, Historic Boulder had recently completed a full renovation of the house. Over the few years preceding the renovation, it released several articles relaying the beautiful and extensive history of Hannah Barker and her legacy. As a result, we decided that we didn't need to include that extensive history—there are enough documents currently circulating that yet another comprehensive chapter on Hannah Barker would just be redundant. So, here it is in shorthand.

A Boulder landmark, the Hannah Barker House is located at 800 Arapahoe and has stood there in some capacity since 1875. The oldest portion was built by Caleb and Carrie Stowell, a childless couple. A widower by the name of Ezra K. Barker purchased the property in the spring of 1877 and moved in with his seven-year-old daughter, Josephine. Half a year later, he met and fell in love with Boulder schoolteacher Hannah Connell. Hannah had emigrated from Ireland at the age of eight; at twenty-three, she arrived in Colorado to teach in Ward and moved to Boulder to become a teacher within the brand-new Boulder Valley School District. Ten years later, she married Ezra and took his name. Over the next six years, the family moved and operated within Boulder's social circles, just as any family would, until Ezra died of consumption (tuberculosis) in early 1883. Consumption was a common cause of death in the nineteenth and early twentieth centuries, although it wasn't identified until 1882, and there was no effective treatment or cure until 1946. Ezra fell victim to the age-old disease, and he left his widow and his child in 800 Arapahoe.

Hannah Barker, an enterprising woman at the still-young age of thirty-three, turned her home into an upscale boardinghouse and rented out the rooms to various tenants. She typically had the help of her adopted daughter, Josie, and one servant at a time. Josie married in the house at the age of twenty-one, and shortly thereafter, Hannah invited a good friend and her sister to join her in the house at 800 Arapahoe. The sister helped Hannah run the boardinghouse until Hannah's death in 1918 of arteriosclerosis (very likely complicated by the influenza pandemic that claimed so many Boulder citizens). She was seventy-four. The house was left to one of the sisters, Mary Davidson, and she died in the house in 1923.

Hannah Barker played a tremendous role Boulder's history. Her house, shown here in circa 1885, is currently undergoing an extensive restoration. *Carnegie Branch Library for Local History, Boulder Historical Society Collection.*

Hannah Barker's life was not limited solely to the management of her boardinghouse; Ezra had left her a significant estate, including both monetary assets and landholdings. It was the management of his vast wealth that created the Hannah Barker still mentioned in Boulder: businesswoman, philanthropist and civic leader. She directed the Boulder National Bank, cofounded the Boulder creamery and founded the Boulder Women's Club. She actively supported a number of other causes, including the Ladies' Literary Society and the Colorado Chautauqua Association, as well as coordinated repairs and grooming for the Columbia Cemetery. She donated the half-block that is currently home to Barker Park and Boulder Day Nursery for use as park grounds and city facilities. In short, she was far more active in her community than most women at the time were expected to be. Her husband taught her everything he knew, and it turned out to be a good investment in their legacies. She is one of the most important Colorado pioneers, highly involved in Boulder's push toward its reputation as a frontier city to be reckoned with. A more extensive history on Hannah and her many accomplishments can be found via the Historic Boulder website.

The physical home of Hannah Barker is almost as grand as her legacy. An unfinished remodel in the 1990s, as well as serious weathering and

Hannah Barker, circa 1869. *Carnegie Branch Library for Local History, Boulder Historical Society Collection.*

unattended aging, somewhat diminished its luster. Now, on the eve of restoration after the house was donated to Historic Boulder in 2010, the building is regaining some of its original grandeur. However, as the dust stirs within these walls, so do the imprints of the people who once dwelled within.

The house was an epicenter for women, creativity and illness—many of its residents died of tuberculosis within its walls, but just as many were influential women in the Boulder community. A published poet was among its denizens, along with many other women of talent and initiative. Some women sought refuge in this house after personal tragedies, like Mary Davidson—she lost her husband and her brother in a short period of time prior to her residence in the house. People suffered within its walls and also found sanctuary there to do good works, both public and personal. Psychics posit that it is the strength of a person's spirit or emotion that makes a haunting more or less likely, and if that is the case, Hannah Barker's house is a logical location for paranormal activity.

Over the course of the renovation—and even for decades before—people have reported seeing faces in the windows of Hannah Barker's house or someone seated on the porch. The presence is undeniably female, but that doesn't necessarily narrow it down to a precise character from the house's history. The hauntings don't begin in the present—Hannah Barker herself seems to have been privy to a spirit that aided her in her entrepreneurial lifestyle: that of her husband.

It has long been said that as long as Hannah lived there, she had the ear of her deceased husband, and he often came through with solutions to any issues that may have arisen regarding the management of his estate or Hannah's life in general. In 2011, the house was included in Historic Boulder's Ghost Walk, Ghost Talk tour. Mary Bell Nyman of Psychic Horizons saw Ezra very clearly as soon as she entered the house. On the first floor, she immediately noted the presence of a male spirit and said, "He died of something, and

I think it was TB…he was mad because he died so young. He wanted to protect his family." Nyman wasn't yet aware of Ezra or Hannah's story, and when she was told just a few moments later, she nodded in affirmation: "He was more eccentric, kind of like an Einstein type…very bright."

As goose bumps appeared on the exposed skin of all parties present, the presence in the Barker House was confirmed—Ezra Barker was there, as he likely had been for 128 years. All paranormal activity at Hannah Barker's house has been muted as of late, as Historic Boulder continues to renovate the structure—understandably, it wishes to focus more on its historical merit than its paranormal activity. However, the whispers still circulate through the neighborhood, and we cannot wait for the house to come to life again and divulge more of its secrets.

REFERENCES

Web Sources

The Arrow of Pi Beta Phi 36, no. 2 (December 1916). Google Books, http://
 bit.ly/15po41q.
Barraco, Jessica. "The Boulderado a Favorite Haunt." *Denver Post.*
 http://www.denverpost.com/ci_7313542.
Boulder History Museum. "Kate Harbeck." http://boulderhistory.org/
 reveal/bios/harbeck.html.
Carter, Laura L. "Coming to Colorado for the Health of It." CU Boulder
 Alumni Association. http://bit.ly/15rriAM.
Colorado Funeral Directors Association. "Funeral Home Directory." http://
 www.cofda.org/Resources/Documents/Colorado-Funeral-Service-
 History-to-1997.pdf.
———. "Our History." http://www.cofda.org/history.
Colorado Paranormal. "Hotel Boulderado/Colorado Paranormal." http://
 coloradoparanormal.tripod.com/hotelboulderado.html.
Denver Public Library Digital Collections. "Hospital at CU Boulder/
 Western History." http://digital.denverlibrary.org/cdm/singleitem/
 collection/p15330coll22/id/9102/rec/36.
The Ditch Project. "150 Years of Ditches: Silver Lake Ditch." http://bcn.
 boulder.co.us/basin/ditchproject/?Our_Ditches:Silver_Lake_Ditch.
Earl, Jim. "Boulder High School/Looking Back," 1978. Boulder High
 School Class of 1965. http://www.bhs65.com/bhs_history_1860/
 looking_back_by_jim_earl.html.

References

Find-a-Grave Memorial. "Charles Edward Kohler (1878–1943)." http://bit.ly/11eijQ8.

ForgottenUSA. "College Inn Is Haunted in Boulder, Colorado." http://bit.ly/119k0gS.

Ghosts of America. "Boulder, Colorado, Ghost Sightings." http://www.ghostsofamerica.com/8/Colorado_Boulder_ghost_sightings.html.

Hall, Mark. "Demolition of Asbestos-Plagued Building on Campus Planned for 2013." Asbestos.com. http://bit.ly/16zaixd.

Haunted Places in the United States and Canada. "Haunt in Boulder College Inn, Haunted Places in Boulder, CO." http://bit.ly/18GSUWU.

———. "Haunt in Boulder High School—Theatre, Haunted Places in Boulder, CO." http://www.hauntin.gs/Boulder-High-School-Theatre_Boulder_Colorado_United-States_151.

Historic Boulder. "The Hannah Barker House." http://www.historicboulder.org/the_hannah_barker_house.html.

———. http://www.historicboulder.org.

Jefferson, Elana A. "Ghost Walk Ghost Talk, a Spirited Tour of Boulder Homes," *Denver Post.* http://www.denverpost.com/athome/ci_19116341.

Lawrence and Gómez Architects. "Masonry at the Edge of Town." http://lawrenceandgomez.wordpress.com/2012/03/25/masonry-at-the-edge-of-town.

Leonard, Stephen J. "The 1918 Influenza Outbreak: An Unforgettable Legacy." *Denver Post.* http://www.denverpost.com/perspective/ci_12268042.

Lewis, Waylan. "The New Tom's Tavern in Boulder, Colorado: A Bradford Heap Local Foodie Restaurant." "Elephant Journal" blog. http://bit.ly/Zl1MMD.

"Longmont FYI." "Haunted Hotel Boulderado," October 21, 2005. Haunted Colorado. http://www.hauntedcolorado.net/Boulder.html.

Macky Auditorium Concert Hall, University of Colorado Boulder. "History." http://macky.colorado.edu/about/history.

Mining Magazine: An International Monthly Review of Current Mining and Metallurgy 7. Google Books, http://bit.ly/12nyOjs.

Pettem, Sylvia. "Arnett-Fullen House Gets New Roof." *Daily Camera.* http://www.dailycamera.com/ci_13092179.

———. "Coroner John Trezise Was the People's Favorite." *Daily Camera.* http://www.dailycamera.com/ci_13066468.

Portrait and Biographical Record of Denver and Vicinity, Colorado…. Chicago, IL: Chapman Publishing Company, 1898. Google Books, http://bit.ly/11vGM2j.

Quarto-centennial Celebration. Boulder: University of Colorado, November 13, 14 and 15, 1902. Google Books, http://bit.ly/11ixw5V.

Remley, Kate, and Dylan Williams, comp. "Arnett-Fullen House." http://www.freewebs.com/arnett-fullenhouse.

Salt Bistro. http://saltboulderbistro.com.

Sample, Tracy, cont. "Memoirs of Ernest Grill, 1886–1902." http://bit.ly/17e2zEe.

Shadowlands. "Haunted Places Index—Colorado." http://theshadowlands.net/places/colorado.htm.

University of Colorado Boulder. "Master Plan." http://www.colorado.edu/masterplan/maps/index.html.

University of Colorado Boulder Heritage Center. "Elaura Jaquette to Be Remembered on Her 61st Birthday." http://cuheritage.org/collections/cu-history/elaura-jaquette-to-be-remembered-on-her-61st-birthday.

———. http://cuheritage.org/exhibits/architecture.

———. "President Joseph A. Sewall." http://cuheritage.org/exhibits/presidents/president-joseph-a-sewall.

University of Colorado Boulder Libraries. "FAQ." http://ucblibraries.colorado.edu/archives/faq.htm.

University of Colorado Boulder, Sewall Residential Academic Program. *University of Colorado Bulletin.* April 12, 1939. http://bit.ly/146Rm5b.

Valenting, Rebecca. "James and Martha Maxwell, Pioneers Extraordinare." "Beyond the Land of Gold" blog. http://bit.ly/18GdHHK.

———. "Pearl Street: Boulder Colorado's Heart." "Beyond the Land of Gold" blog. http://bit.ly/10HhmDe.

Varnell, Jeanne. *Women of Consequence: The Colorado Women Hall of Fame.* Boulder, CO: Johnson Books, 1999. Google Books, http://bit.ly/146Psl8.

Wallace, Alicia. "New Beginning for Tom's Tavern Site." *Daily Camera.* http://www.dailycamera.com/ci_13226063.

Welcome to Boulder History Museum. "Andrew J. Macky (1834–1907)." http://boulderhistory.org/macky.asp.

Wikipedia. "Boulder High School." http://en.wikipedia.org/wiki/Boulder_High_School.

———. "Colorado Central Railroad." http://en.wikipedia.org/wiki/Colorado_Central_Railroad.

———. "History of Colorado." http://en.wikipedia.org/wiki/History_of_Colorado.

———. "Hotel Boulderado." http://en.wikipedia.org/wiki/Hotel_Boulderado.

———. "Joseph Sewall." http://en.wikipedia.org/wiki/Joseph_Sewall.

———. "Theodore Dru Alison Cockerell." http://en.wikipedia.org/wiki/Theodore_Dru_Alison_Cockerell.

———. "University of Colorado Boulder." http://en.wikipedia.org/wiki/University_of_Colorado_Boulder.

Wise, Carolyn C., Stephanie Hauser and Vault staff, eds. *The College Buzz Book, 2007.* New York: Vault Career Library, 2007. Google Books, http://bit.ly/17JCLR5.

Books/Periodicals/Documents

Arnett, R.E. "History of Arnett Hotel Told by Son of Its Founder." *Daily Camera,* June 29, 1940.

Barker, Jane Valentine. "Home Mortuary to Office Building." *Daily Camera,* June 15, 1975.

———. *76 Boulder Historic Homes.* Boulder, CO: Pruett Publishing, 1976.

Boulder City Planning Department. *2305 Broadway Street Historic Building Inventory Record.* Boulder, CO: self-published, 1986.

Boulder Landmarks Preservation Advisory Board. *Frederick Kohler Jr. House Landmark Designation Papers.* Boulder, CO: self-published, 1992.

Brown, Roz, and Ann Alexander Leggett. *Haunted Boulder: Ghostly Tales from the Foot of the Flatirons.* Boulder, CO: White Sand Lake Press, 2002.

———. *Haunted Boulder 2: Ghostly Tales from Boulder and Beyond.* Boulder, CO: White Sand Lake Press, 2003.

Broysky, Cindy. "Historic Group Hopes to Scare Up Funds with Ghostly Tour on Halloween Weekend." *Daily Camera,* October 27, 1999.

Daily Camera. "George Hall's Death Recalls Corpse Swindle." September 10, 1960.

———. "George R.A. Hall, Former Boulder Leader, Dies." September 8, 1960.

———. "O.P. Pherson Nears 90th Year, Will Be Featured in New Book." November 15, 1971.

———. "Remodeling Transforms Old Mansion." November 18, 1972.

Denver Republican. "Stood Over Bathtub While His Lifeblood Ebbed Away." October 14, 1904.

Kohler Family Clippings Collection, 1923–69, BHS 328-151-41. BPL Carnegie Library for Local History.

O.P. Pherson Papers, 1881–1977, BHS 328-185. BPL Carnegie Library for Local History.